# FLIPPING HOUSES

*Real Estate Make Money Guide - How to Find, Buy, Fix and Flip Residential Properties*

**ALLEN CAIN**

# TABLE OF CONTENTS

# INTRODUCTION

F lipping refers to purchasing an asset for the purpose of selling it for a quick profit rather than continuing long-term evaluation.

Flipping is used to describe some investor activities in short-term real estate transactions and initial public offerings (IPOs).

While these are the most common uses in finance, flipping can be used to describe the purchase of assets that are intended to be sold in the short term for profit, including cars, cryptocurrencies, concert tickets, etc. The Flipping is most closely related to real estate and refers to the strategy of buying real estate and selling it for a short period of time (usually within a year).

In real estate, flipping is usually classified into one of two types. The first type is a resale that targets real estate in a market that is being valued rapidly by real estate investors with little or no additional investment in physical assets. This is a play for the market situation, not the real estate itself.

The second type is quick-fix flips, where real estate investors use the knowledge that they want to improve undervalued real estate through renovations and cosmetic changes and resell for a greater value and make a profit.

Although flipping has brought great benefits to real estate, it appears that it produces more infomercials than the easily replicated results.

A reversal in the hot market makes these two risks higher because the hot market can cool unexpectedly. If market conditions change before selling real estate, real estate investors will remain depreciable assets.

The reversal after improving undervalued real estate is less dependent on market timing, but market conditions may still play a role. Investors need to inject additional capital into their investments to increase asset value beyond purchases, refurbishments, carry costs, and closing costs.

House flipping sounds simple and easy in principle, but it requires more than an easy understanding of real estate in a profitable way.

# CHAPTER ONE
# WHAT IS HOUSE FLIPPING

House flipping usually means that after repairs or improvements are made, the house is purchased and resold for profit. The definition of "quickly" varies. Put it within 6 months.

Overall, it means buying a home that is going to be profitable and resold soon. This is a popular activity in the hot real estate market, especially among professional real estate brokers.

This is a quick profit strategy where investors buy real estate at discounted prices and improve real estate to sell at higher prices. If the housing market is strong, this is a very profitable strategy.

Old homes and mortgages are popular properties used in overturning homes because investors can get these properties fairly cheaply, increasing potential profits. In some cases, contractors are used to doing real estate upgrades, but experienced house flippers may do the work themselves.

Many market dealers do the same thing but keep buyers and sellers in stock shortly to provide faster transactions, but this has never been seen very favorably. But middlemen never get good news.

Nevertheless, if the house price is lowered, investors who turn over the house are at risk of losing money on the investment just as the profit may be huge when house prices go up.

## Does House Flipping Works Today

Turning over the house may sound easy, but not as easy as it looks. Let's become a reality. House flips are both dreams and disasters.

If done the right way, house flips are a big investment. In a short time, you can make a smart renovation and sell your home for much more than you paid for it.

However, house flips can go in the wrong direction if done in the wrong way. I've heard a horror story that turns the house over. It looks like a house with a rocking base and a leaking roof that turns out to look good. At the end of the day, turning the house over may not make you money. It actually costs thousands.

If you decide to turn the house over, you certainly don't want to lose money. You want to make wise investments and earn rewards. Without advanced knowledge of the local real estate market, you can't turn a house over.

The only way to know if a particular property is really a deal is if you know the market value of an equivalent house in the area.

You will have all the time needed to get a real estate license so that you can access the local multiple listing service. This has two advantages. You have access to both price offerings and sales, and you can recognize it as soon as it is on the market, to help you find real bargains.

Must be purchased at WELL under the dominant market, never disregard this procedure. If you consider the final selling price of a property as a retail price, the price you pay is considered a wholesale price. The difference between the two should provide ample benefits and room to cover property refurbishment.

When buying a reversing house, you can't buy based on emotional factors (I really like this property). Your success depends almost entirely on the numbers, and you must absolutely forgive them.

## How much can I earn flipping houses

Real estate data company ATTOM reported that the average profit for House flipping in the US in the second quarter of 2018 was $ 65,520.

However, ATTOM considers all housing sold or sold within one year (with or without real estate), and only considers the purchase price minus the sales price. Experienced flippers will tell you that they are not the only important numbers.

A single house flip averages about $ 30,000, which is fairly accurate for most house flippers: the numbers decrease for low price flips and increase for high end flips.

The amount of money earned from corrections and flips depends on the value of each transaction and the house. You can set a goal for each fix and make a profit of at least $ 25,000.

There are many risks associated with repairing or turning your house over. You should not trade if there is no potential profit of at least $ 25,000. The higher the house, the more risks, and costs, then you can make more money.

You can also determine how much profit you need for the work you need. For homes that require major remodeling, you will want to earn more than $ 30,000. In a house that only needs painting and carpet, the work is easy and quick, so it can accept a small margin.

## Disadvantages of House Flipping

IF HOUSE FLIPS ARE PROFITABLE, THE TAX WILL BE HIGHER.

"Flipping" is a term that refers to selling a house before closing it, basically by having someone pay to assign a purchase contract. However, most people use this term more commonly to refer to buying a home and reselling it at a higher price. You can make some money when it works, but tipping comes at a cost.

RISK OF LOSING MONEY

One of the biggest drawbacks of flipping the house is that it doesn't always work. If you can't resell your purchase agreement, you may lose your deposit when you back out or you may have trouble buying an unplanned home.

Buy, rehab, and sell flips can result in lost money if rehabilitation is higher than expected, if the market shifts downward, or if the buyer is not interested in the house.

OPPORTUNITY COST

If you succeed in flip transactions, you can probably get quite a deal when you first contract a house. If you flip it, you regain capital and profits, but you need to reinvest that money.

Holding real estate purchased as rentals can sometimes generate sound monthly cash flows. Reversing it means missing the opportunity to collect that ongoing income stream.

# Part-Time House Flipping

There is a complete chance for a part-time house flipping. As a matter of fact there is little or no difference between the full-time house flipping or part-time.

REASONS TO FLIP HOUSES PART TIME

**Looking for Extra Income** – Flipping 1 or 2 houses a year can be a great way to make some additional income on the side.

**Busy Schedule or Lack of Time** – Someone with a busy schedule might choose to flip a few houses as opposed to flipping none at all.

**Enjoy Current Full-Time Job** – Some flippers choose to flip part-time because they already have a full-time job they love or enjoy they don't want to leave.

**Just Getting Started** – As mentioned above flipping houses part-time is a great way to get started in the business.

**Lack of Resources** – Flipping houses requires a lot of resources and capital and many people only have enough resources or capital to flip one house at the time.

# Pitfalls to Avoid When Flipping Houses Part-Time

While flipping houses part-time is possible and can offer many great benefits there are some pitfalls and traps that you must be careful to avoid when flipping part-time.

The first thing to remember is that part-time house flipping doesn't mean there is any less work required in flipping a house.

House flipping requires a lot of time and energy and just because you choose to pursue flipping part-time doesn't mean there is any less work or effort involved.

The biggest difference between part-time and full-time house flipping is not the amount of work involved but how long the work takes.

One of the biggest problems and challenges in flipping houses part-time is the potential for gaps in market knowledge, which can lead to poor decisions and potential losses when flipping houses.

Keep in mind that just because it's been many months since you last flipped a house that doesn't mean the real estate market has stayed frozen in time.

The real estate market and housing prices are always in a constant state of change and flux. So when flipping houses part-time, it's important to stay informed and up to date about your local real estate market.

### TIPS WHEN FLIPPING HOUSES ON THE SIDE

**Make a schedule and stick with it** – When flipping houses part-time. It's easy to get off track or let an entire week go by without getting anything accomplished. While you might move at a slower pace it's still important to keep the house flip moving forward.

**Have Appropriate Expectations** – Don't expect full-time results with part-time efforts. If you plan to flip houses part-time don't expect to make a fortune. While house-flipping can be a great side income, as with any business you get out of it what you put in.

**Always Stay Current on the Real Estate Market** – Just because you choose to flip houses part-time doesn't mean you don't need to know the same information that a full-time house flipper knows.

**Keep a Close Eye on Contractors** – When flipping houses part-time and using contractors or subcontractors don't assume things are getting done in your absence. It's important to check on your flip every day or at least every other day to make sure work is getting done on time and correctly.

**Consider Hiring a Project Manager** – As a part-time house flipper, you might not always be able to be on the job site. So if the budget allows for one, you might want to consider hiring a project manager that can be there in your stead.

**Check on the Property Routinely** – When flipping houses, part-time don't forget to check on your house flips on a regular basis. When a house is sitting empty things can often go wrong such as water leaks or vandalism, so it's important to go by the property at regular intervals to ensure the property is in stable condition and secure.

**Always Keep an Eye Out for the Next Flip** – When flipping part-time it's easy to slack off on looking for your next house flip. Remember though whether flipping houses part-time or full time, finding inventory is the lifeblood of any successful house flipping business.

# CHAPTER TWO
# TAXES AND IMPLICATIONS

In general, housing reversals are not considered a passive investment by IRS. The tax rules define flipping as "active income" and the profits of the flipped house are treated as regular income with a tax rate of 10% to 37%, not a capital gain of 0% to 20%. The Taxes on house reversals usually include self-employment taxes.

If an investor is classified as a "dealer" by the IRS, the profit from the real estate flip is taxed at the normal income tax rate. Profit is calculated by subtracting the cost, including the purchase price from the final sale price. Tax rates for "active investors" who are earning positive profits range from 10% to 37%.

According to the IRS, property dealers purchase property and sell it to customers "in the normal course of business or business." Most fixed investors are considered dealers.

They hold assets in the short term, and most of their income comes from turning the house over. Even real estate investors who occasionally turn over their homes are usually considered dealers and are taxed at their normal income rate.

On the contrary, profits from real estate held over 12 months are usually subject to more favorable long-term capital gain brackets in the range of 0% to 20%. Investors can choose to rent or occupy the asset.

**Normal Income Tax Results When Turning the House Over**

If classified as a dealer, the profit from the flip is taxed at the normal rate of income. Currently, the normal income tax rate is 10% to 37%. In addition, profits are subject to self-employment tax (equivalent to self-employed FICA). This is 15.3%, twice the amount normally paid for W2 employees.

As a dealer, Flip's total tax ranges from a minimum of 25.3% to a maximum of 52.3%, depending on the tax rate. Needless to say, you don't want to misunderstand that your interests are completely yours.

**When Capital Gains Tax Applies To Flipping Houses**

By avoiding the dealer definition and fortunately gaining from selling the house after turning the house upside down most of year after year, the profit from the sale is taxed at a low capital gain rate.

Note that this is rare for most flippers. Most of the time, they are taxed at the normal income tax rate, but I would like to mention that it happens. Even better, if you are eligible for capital gains tax, you do not have to pay self-employment tax.

**Short-Term Capital Gains House Flipping Tax**

If the property is held for less than 12 months, there will be no incentive for profits from Flip. Short-term capital gains are taxed at the normal income tax rate, whether defined as a dealer or an investor. However, there is an advantage of not paying 15.3% self-employment tax, so you can still save a lot.

## Long-Term Capital Gain House Flipping Tax

If the asset is held for more than one year and is not classified as a dealer, the profit from the flip is taxed according to the long-term capital gain rate. Currently, these tax rates range from 0% to 20% for most taxpayers. Compared to a normal income tax rate and a one-to-two punch of self-employment tax, you can save a lot.

## How to Calculate Taxes For Inverted Houses

Eventually, you will be taxed on fixed-price profits. This is the selling price minus total costs and deductions. Profit is calculated by subtracting the cost, including the purchase price from the final sale price.

## Purchase Amount

The purchase price includes the cost of the house itself. Although closing expenses, points, etc. may be considered part of the purchase price, to make accounting easier, it is best to treat everything except the actual purchase of the building itself as expenses.

When considering what your profits are, consider only the purchase price, not the amount financed in the profit equation. IRS does not consider funding when calculating profits. However, you can deduct interest paid as expenses.

## Expense

Expenses that exceed the purchase price include mortgage interest and points, loan fees, materials and supplies, labor, closure costs, taxes, professional services, and all marketing and real estate agent fees associated with the sale of real estate. The

As the purchase price, the IRS is not worried about how to pay for the costs. As long as the cost is related to the asset, it is usually deductible. For example, if you charge $ 10,000 to a building materials lows credit card, it is considered a property renovation fee.

## Home Repair and Turnover Costs

### Profit

Profit is the amount settled on sale after all costs, including purchase price have been taken into account. you can put yourself in a better position by having a good record of your expenses to ensure you deduct all renovation expenses. The basic formula is Transaction profit = sale price-purchase price-cost.

Remember when calculating your profits to report that the IRS may not be your actual profits. For example, if you have to repay a mortgage loan that you used to raise funds for purchases and refurbishment, you'll end up with takeaway funds. This amount can be estimated using the following formula: Selling price-Mortgage-Expense = Bringing home profit to investors

### Annual Tax

From there, multiplying the taxable income by the normal income tax rate will result in an estimated annual tax burden. Keep in mind that you can use other corrections and flip losses completed in the same year to offset the profit.

**How to submit and pay your home to turn over taxes**

After calculating the flipping house tax, you need to know when to submit and how to pay. In general, if you are registered as a sole proprietor, part of LLC, or company S, and the home turning business makes more than $ 1,000 a year, you must pay quarterly taxes.

If you haven't generated any revenue or meet other exemptions, you'll report taxes at the end of the year. However, most home flips pay quarterly taxes. These quarterly taxes are known as estimated taxes and are usually paid by April 15, June 15, September 15, and January 15 each year.

For example, if you turn your house over from January 1st to March 31st, your income is April 15th. However, if these dates fall on weekends or holidays, you will be taxed for the next business day.

## How to Save House Flipping Tax

While it is difficult to avoid the basic considerations of flipping as an active income, there are some special cases that are not subject to the usual income tax and that help to flip property. These include continuing to invest for longer periods and owning property as your primary residence.

**Here Are Few Ways To Reduce Taxes When Turning The House Over.**

**Holding Investment Property for More Than 1 Year**

If you find yourself in a category that can pay capital gains tax instead of regular income tax, predict whether retaining the property for over a year will work. Please note that if you own more than one year, you will be charged a long-term capital gain tax, not a short-term.

**Make the Main Residence Before Overturning The Property**

If a property is casually turned over, consider whether you can move into that property as your primary residence after the renovation is complete. Moving to real estate may change the tax considerations for the final sale from active income to capital gains. In addition, current tax laws may completely avoid taxing profits if you live in this property for two of the five years prior to sale.

**Perform A Tax Postponed Exchange of Flip**

The tax deferral exchange, also known as the 1031 exchange, allows you to carry the profits of one property to another property. To qualify for this, you must hold a property for at least one year (which is better from an IRS perspective) and lease it to a tenant. It cannot be used only with the Quick Turn property.

**Billing House Flipping Tax Credit**

IRS allows house flippers to amortize certain costs associated with the purchase, renovation, and sale of real estate. Offsetting these costs helps reduce taxable income. You can deduct some costs before switching properties, but you cannot deduct other costs, such as capital expenditure until the property is sold.

## Costs That Can Be Deducted When Turning Over the House

It is important to know the costs that can be deducted when turning the house over. This will tell you how much your taxable income will be, so you can secure money to pay taxes. This will affect your budget for your next flip.

## Costs That Can Be Deducted When Turning The House Upside Down Include:

Capital expenditure (expenses related to buying and refurbishing a house to be turned over). These are subtracted after inverting the properties.

- Vehicle costs. This includes gasoline and repair costs, or standard mileage.
- Office expenses including rent, utility charges, office supplies such as printer ink and paper
- Building permit
- Mortgage interest

## TYPES OF REAL ESTATE FINANCING

Acquiring the right type of loan can increase purchasing power, ultimately increase cash flow, and increase return on investment. However, borrowers can easily be overwhelmed because there is a variety of real estate lending options to select, investigate, and evaluate from literally thousands of lenders.

So what are the common options for real estate finance? Which option is best for you? Below are some ways to configure real estate transactions and examples of when to use them.

## Conventional Loan

If you move into a house that doesn't need repairs and you have fair credit, a traditional loan is a good choice.

Traditional mortgages consider the following information about the borrower:

- Credit score
- Assets
- income
- debt

Buyers usually need to pay a down payment of five to twenty-five percent of the purchase price. Traditional loans must meet strict guidelines (as set by investment giants Fannie Mae and Freddie Mac) before being issued. However, borrowers typically benefit from low-interest rates because the risks associated with traditional loans are low.

## Blanket Loan

Builders and property developers often look for these loans as an alternative to individual loans for land parcels or multiple properties. Comprehensive loans are used to fund multiple real estates, larger lands, or land that are ultimately segmented and sold. A comprehensive loan allows the borrower to sell a portion of the property without retiring the entire mortgage.

## Portfolio Loan

Those who struggle to meet the stringent requirements closely associated with traditional loans can rely on portfolio lenders. Anyone who purchases real estate that doesn't have an acceptable credit rating or does not meet the criteria of the category can consider this option.

A portfolio loan is a mortgage held in a bank portfolio. They are not sold in the secondary market and does not need to comply with underwriting guidelines set by secondary market investors. Portfolio lenders are more flexible in terms of portfolio loan terms but often charge higher interest rates. Portfolio loans are ideal for borrowers who are outside the scope of standard mortgage underwriting guidelines.

## Hard Money Loan

Hard money loans are often used to purchase real estate that has poor conditions and requires repair. Unlike traditional mortgages, hard money loans are supported by private funds from individuals or funds from wealthy investors.

Requirement regulations are relaxed, so hard money loans can be protected quickly. Many real estate investors are looking for large loans for a quick turnaround. The lender agrees to do the transaction based on the value of the property, not the buyer's credit, debt, income, assets.

These types of loans are ideal for real estate flippers and other investors but can be expensive. The interest rate of hard money loans is very high compared to conventional loans. It is important to have a strategy on how to terminate a hard money loan and plan to secure a long-term loan at a low-interest rate after a certain period of months.

**Piggy Bank**

This type of real estate finance, sometimes referred to as a "piggyback" or combo (combo) loan, can be used when the borrower does not pay the full twenty percent required to avoid paying private mortgage insurance (PMI) .

Also, wealthy clients can be used to maintain the first mortgage under the restrictions of Fannie Mae and Freddie Mac to avoid jumbo interest rates. The buyer must pay fifteen percent of the purchase price and split the remainder into a first mortgage with eighty percent of the price and a second mortgage with five percent of the price.

 The second number represents the second mortgage, and the third number represents the down payment.

# FINANCING OPTION SUMMARY

| Financing Types | Loan Amounts | Interest Rates | Repayment Terms | Turnaround Time | Credit Criteria |
|---|---|---|---|---|---|
| SBA Loans | $50,000 – $5 million | 6% – 13% | 5 – 25 years | 30 days – 6 months | Usually requires a minimum business credit score (FICO SBSS) |
| Traditional Bank Loans | $250,000 + | 5% – 10% | 1 – 20 years | 2 – 4 months | Usually requires strong personal and/or business credit scores |
| Online Loans | $25,000 – $500,000 | 7% – 30% | 1 – 5 years | 2 – 7 days | Less important, but still a main factor |
| Micro-Loans | $500 – $50,000 | 8% – 15% | 1 – 5 years | 1 – 3+ months | Less important, but still a main factor |
| Merchant Cash Advance | $200 – $250,000 | 15% – 150% | 3 – 12 months | 1 – 7 days | Not required |
| Cash Flow Loans | $200 – $100,000 | 25% – 90% | 6 – 12 months | Minutes – 3 days | Less important, but still a factor |

| Business Credit Cards | $250 – $25,000 | 13% 25% | 30 days | 1 – 3 weeks | Personal and/or business credit are a main factor. |
|---|---|---|---|---|---|
| Vendor Financ- ing | $1,000 – $100,000 | 0 – 36% | 10 – 120 days | Hours to weeks | Usually requires good business credit scores |

# TIPS FOR SUCCESSFUL BORROWING

So you need the money, and you are thinking about asking for a loan for your flipping business here are tips before asking for a loan.

### Analyze If You Really Need It

Asking money from either a relative or a bank is nothing that should be taken lightly. Remember that when you ask for money, the ideal is to return it and even with interest, so try to analyze if before reaching that option you have others.

### Investigate All Options

Many people, when asking for a loan the first thing they do is go to their favorite bank and take it directly from there, without first evaluating other options. Before requesting a loan you investigate what other banks can offer you, or even look for different ways.

Nowadays, you can apply for loans online, on different platforms, so there are no excuses to investigate and learn more before making any decision.

### Try To Look For a Fixed Rate

I never liked the variable word very much. It's true, and it may vary down, but what if he did it up. If possible, try to ask for a fixed-rate loan, so you really know the amount you will be paying each month, and you will not get any other surprises along the way.

### Be Careful With the Deadline

Let's assume you are going to ask for a loan for a venture. Then you should keep in mind that the term for the loan payment is not less than the time in which you expect your venture to work.

Otherwise, you will reach that deadline and possibly without having completed the payments as you should.

### Have All the Papers Up To Date

Many people at the time of requesting a loan, begin to catch up with their papers to discover that finally, the process becomes delinquent, bureaucratic and even expensive because sometimes you have to take out certain roles that we did not know.

## CHAPTER THREE
## WHERE YOU SHOULD BUY

There are considered factors in the choice of areas to flip houses. It is difficult to choose the most profitable market because the market trends change yearly.

So to build wealth as an investor, you need to spend a lot of time on thorough research. The best place to turn the house over is not always obvious, and there are various factors to consider.

In addition, some markets that were temporarily excellent places to flip the house eventually became concentrated and no longer desirable. For this reason, the smartest investor spends time discovering promising areas to flip the house, rather than jumping into existing trends.

Markets, where the unemployment rate is low or declining, should be considered very much, coupled with significant employment growth. These factors may be driven by the arrival of fast-growing industries and notable companies in the region. Both are signs of economic improvement that drive home purchase activity and the ultimate rise in asset value.

It is also important to note whether there are nice neighborhoods in areas where people want to live. Finally, it is important to ensure that there is sufficient inventory in the market.

Once these factors are met, you can focus on financial factors such as median purchase price and local average labor and retrofit costs. These numbers help investors to calculate the post-repair value (ARV) and profit margin estimates.

It is important to note due diligence in this regard, as strong economic indicators do not automatically match favorable conditions for housing flippers. However, if you identify a market that promises strong economic growth and profitable profit margins, you can be confident in starting a property search.

## DETERMINE YOUR FARM AREA

The best place to turn the house over is not necessarily the city with the highest potential for profit, but where you can make valuable profits everywhere.

The top three markets that reversed housing in 2018 were South Dakota, Indiana, and Texas.

The best market for turning homes usually suggests a profit margin that is worth the admission fee.

One of the best ways to do this is to look at trends from the past to predict where the housing market will next take us. According to Attom Data Solutions, last year, US housing flippers earned an average gross profit of over $ 65,000 per property.

However, be aware that profitability can vary greatly from place to place, and the top market changes from year to year. Below is a review of the cities that are considered the most desirable to overturn housing in the past few years. Can you forecast the top market in 2019?

## EL PASO, TEXAS

El Paso, Texas is at the top of the list of great places to turn homes in 2018. This is due to its remarkable market potential. According to U.S. News, Texas's locale is 7.2 out of 10 in terms of quality of life, ranking it as the fifth retirement place in the United States.

According to Zillow, more than 70 Fortune 500 companies are based in the region and are considered the fourth largest manufacturing base in the United States. The median home price was $ 123,400, an increase of 3.6% over the previous year.

These statistics, coupled with low renovation and retrofit costs in the region, provided investors with a large return on investment potential.

## OKLAHOMA CITY, OKLAHOMA

Oklahoma City is known as a regional economic center in various fields such as information technology, medical services, and government. Oklahoma City regained the top spot in real estate rankings due to very reasonable home renovation and renovation costs and good quality of life.

Oklahoma City is the best metropolis to start a business, a key indicator of economic, population and housing growth

## PEORIA, ARIZONA

This Arizona city is one of the cheapest places to renovate and remodel assets in the country, and the median home price has steadily increased over the past six years.

## SIOUX FALLS, SOUTH DAKOTA

Called "America's Best Little City," Sioux Falls is a spotlight on low-cost home remodeling and relatively low home prices ($183,500). It is characterized by many prominent financial companies and a solid regional medical industry.

The place was promising, with a great quality of life and an 8.8% increase in home value in just one year.

## WHAT YOU SHOULD BUY

In Flipping houses, the target should be to buy at a very low price and repair to sell at a profit. Buying houses that are low in price will require you to fix such house before putting it up for sale. These are the type of low purchase houses you should target and buy.

### Distressed Properties

The key to success in flipping the house is to find the tormented property. Defective properties are usually priced based on market prices, and sometimes require foreclosure or some work.

Property owners may find it difficult to find because they hate to call their home suffered. However, research can help you find the gem you are looking for.

Here are ways to find distressed characteristics:

## *ABANDONED HOUSE OR UNOCCUPIED HOUSE*

It may be difficult to find, but every city has a vacant house. There are several reasons why the property is vacant, and each can present an opportunity for you.

**Out-of-town owner**: The owner moved to another town and left the property empty rather than trying to rent or sell it. It may not simply be a priority for them.

**Bank-owned real estate**: This Real Estate has been seized, and many of this real estate is vacant. Banks are very interested in obtaining real estate balances, so you can usually get quite a lot.

**Government property**: Like property owned by banks, these are the result of foreclosure and can be found on government websites.

**Will test**: In the case of a homeowner who is dead and the heir is not local or has no spouse, and the facility may be vacant and open for sale. You can find probation properties at the county registrar.

## *DELINQUENT OWNERS*

Arrears can be either tax or mortgage payments.

**Mortgage arrears**: Once you receive a foreclosure document, many owners abandon their homes because they cannot pay their arrears.

**Tax**: If the property is seized with unpaid tax and the owner is evicted, it will remain empty until the municipality decides to auction. These properties can be found at the tax assessor's office.

## LISTINGS

You can find real estate that sells below market value with MLS search, but it is very rare in some markets. Another option is to look at a site that lists the homes sold by the owner.

Look at local newspapers with Craigslist to find a house like this. These sellers are quite motivated to get rid of their assets immediately.

## SENIOR CITIZENS

Older owners can no longer maintain their homes, often trying to move to something smaller and easier to maintain. Most of them are open to direct marketing campaigns, and you can find seniors from direct mailing companies.

There are many ways to find distressed assets, network with people, and let them know what you do. Keep an eye out because you will find something when you travel around town before you know it.

## PRE FORECLOSURES AND THE NOTICE OF DEFAULT

After a landlord does not meet your mortgage payments, the lender will first send a Notice of Default, informing you of the amount due and granting you a certain period in which you can pay.

If the owner does not pay for that date, a troubled property sale will be scheduled for your property. The Notice of Default marks the beginning of the pre-foreclosure period.

The owner can interrupt the execution at any time before the sale date by paying the total amount due on loan, so several owners decide to sell their properties in difficulties on their own.

This allows them to avoid foreclosure, which could have a very important long-term effect on your credit. But, as the owner of the property must only pay the remaining debt on loan and not the total amount, they can sell their property for less than the total value to secure the sale, and still get enough money to cover their debt.

This leads to great discounts for buyers and investors and great opportunities for homeowners in difficulties who wish to avoid foreclosure.

## *AUCTIONS AND SALES OF PROPERTIES IN DIFFICULTIES*

If the homeowner does not sell the property before the date scheduled for sale as foreclosure, the property will be sold at a public auction by the lender or someone you trust.

The foreclosure auctions or houses difficulties are the most common way by which buyers get foreclosed properties for sale. These auctions occur all the time throughout the country and are undoubtedly one of the most direct ways to buy real estate of any kind.

All you have to do is show up on auction day and be ready to bid, and if you are the winner, the property will be yours. Of course there is a great preparation to buy houses for low prices in a foreclosure auction.

You must ensure the financing in advance to be able to pay the amount for the winning offer, and you must do a thorough investigation about the repossessed properties that you want to buy to be sure that they are good, and a valuable investment.

But whether you are an expert in the purchase of houses for sale, land for sale or properties in certified difficulties or a novice buyer, the auction process is very different from that of a typical real estate sale.

You will not have to negotiate with an agent, and you will receive a Sales Invoice as soon as the auction ends. It is a fantastic way to buy a property or houses at the auction up to 60% below the market value, and the discounts will be higher than you can find anywhere else.

### *REO HOUSING AND BANK OWNED HOUSES*

If a foreclosure auction does not find a buyer, or the winning bid is below a certain "minimum bid" amount set by the auctioneer, then the property will be delivered to the lender at the end of the auction.

The lender, usually a bank or a government agency, will then take full control over the property and place it for sale by itself.

These properties are called bank property or REO (real estate owned). Almost all banks offer reclaimed homes, but the problem is that they generally do not have time to advertise or market these properties.

Instead, they let local agents show the houses for sale. Buy properties in difficulty for sale, Home sales, as well as REO, offer the same incredible discounts as any other real estate investment with difficulties.

Banks usually sell these properties below their real price just to get rid of them, and people or investors who want to buy a house will find excellent offers there.

# THE FORECLOSURE PROCESS

Before you start buying foreclosure homes, you need to know what foreclosure is. This is the process by which a lender attempts to collect the outstanding amount from a delinquent mortgage.

When the property owner does not meet his loan installments, the lender has the right to regain its home to guarantee the loan. Next is the time when you can choose to buy foreclosures or foreclosure homes.

This is a simple problem. If a mortgage is granted, the house itself acts as collateral, so if the payment is not met correctly, the house is sold or auctioned by the lender.

## UNDERSTANDING THE FORECLOSURE PROCESS

### STEP 1: HOW DOES FORECLOSURE BEGINS

Foreclosure Initiation The foreclosure process usually begins when a homeowner or borrower fails to meet a mortgage payment. When this happens, depending on the pending installments, the lender can choose to request debt payments within a certain period of time, and if this is not met, foreclosure begins.

To begin the foreclosure process, the lender must submit public payment requirements to the debtor. This official requirement, known as a default or litigation notice, is essential to prove that the debtor is aware of the debt owed to the lender.

If you want to buy this type of home, you can find a big advantage over the free market, but before buying a home with foreclosure, you know how the sales process for this type of home works It is necessary to keep. You need the information you need to search for these types of properties and know very well what the current value is.

## STEP 2: FORECLOSURE PROCESS

If homeowners who are aware of unpaid debt before foreclosure cannot pay the payment, they can choose to sell the house before foreclosure takes place.

In this case, we are talking about the fact that the owner can sign a sales contract with the buyer at the sale.

In this way, he avoids having a bad record of foreclosure in his credit history, so pre-seizure is a great advantage for the borrower or default homeowner. This is really important for future operations as it will be difficult to raise new funds in the future with foreclosure and past foreclosure.

If you want to buy advance foreclosures, you can get a big discount because the selling price is usually 20-60% lower than the market price. This is a big advantage for those who want to buy a house or make a good investment for the future. Another advantage is that you can know in advance everything related to the property title and avoid future unpleasant surprises.

## STEP 3: FORECLOSURE AUCTION

If the pre-execution period for the mortgage auction mortgage expires, but the outstanding loan is not repaid, the lender will continue to process the mortgage.

From this point on, the property will be offered in a public auction so potential buyers can bid.

Residential auctions usually cover the debt that exists in real estate. In that case, the process ends with payment to the lender, and the house becomes the asset of the successful bidder.

To understand the foreclosure property auction process, the first thing we must do is to differentiate between judicial auctions and extra-legal auctions, as each state establishes its own rules in this regard.

It is essential to know what rules govern the state you are bidding on.

When bidding on an auction, the first thing you should do is find out which houses are participating in the auction in the state where you want to find the property. A good option for this is to look for frequently published and updated lists.

The auction bidding process can be very complex, so you need to get enough information. In many cases, if you bid on a house, you will be asked to prepay part or the entire house, so make sure you have the necessary money or funds.

An important factor to consider in an auction is to fully evaluate the value of the property so that you do not pay much beyond the actual value of the property. If you don't want to pay more than you expect, mark your maximum bid, and don't bid higher.

One drawback is that there are few options for inspecting properties or searching for property titles. Therefore, you should consult an expert on these issues.

## STEP 4: BANK OR GOVERNMENT ASSET RECOVERY (REO)

It should be noted that both banks and some government agencies may be the owners of unpaid loans, and therefore all of them can perform foreclosure.

That said, it's worth knowing that your auction bid may be significantly below your outstanding debt or you may not have a bid. In these cases, either a government or bank lender may decide to leave the auction and collect the property for inclusion in the property portfolio. This is a phase of the process called REO.

If a lender is forced to recover its property due to default, the most reasonable thing is to sell it again to face an unpaid debt. In this case, the real estate agent sells bank or government assets and looks for buyers who are willing to pay the price to avoid lender losses.

One advantage of acquiring this type of asset from a bank or government is that the house is in very good condition, usually because it invests in the necessary repairs and improvements. This kind of improvement can increase the selling price, but the profits that can be achieved are somewhat lower.

## BENEFITS OF BUYING A FORECLOSURE HOME

If you decide to invest in this type of housing, keep in mind that there are multiple benefits.

The first is the possibility of getting good real estate at a much more affordable price in the real estate market than the store price.

You can also negotiate with the buyer in advance on the best conditions for both you and you to win.

If your idea is to invest in making a profit from the sale of real estate in the future, buying a foreclosure home is definitely the best option. Consider the low price you can make foreclosed home purchases and think about the profits you can get in future sales.

# CHAPTER FOUR
# PROPERTY CRITERIA

### COMFORTABLE UNDERGROUND SALES PRICE

The natural thing to do when taking a flip is to look at the top comp. "Oh, it's selling for $ 800,000, and the property is only 500 square feet, so it'll sell for $ 795,000!"

The problem is that you need to prepare for the worst-case scenario. Is there a comp next to the $ 800,000 house just sold for $ 500,000? Upon further review, is it really similar to this theme?

Yes, I know, your flips look much nicer than those sold for $ 550,000! You may be told, "There is nothing even comparable!" Anyway, the $ 550,000 Comp shows a comfortable underground selling price for the flip. I'm not saying it will sell for $ 550,000, but if things don't work, make sure your house sells at least that much.

This is not necessarily a transaction killer, especially if you buy the target house for $ 300,000 or something. However, to build or make the deal work, you need to resell anything over $ 550,000. Yes, it may work, but in the worst case, I know that this transaction will profit with a number of $ 550,000.

## "POP" POTENTIAL

Now that all the comfortable basement numbers have been set let's see if there is a big upside possibility. (Note: There is a reason why a comfortable underground sales price comes before this.)

That $ 800,000 comp is definitely good for your target property. Even better, have two other couples in the $ 700,000 range. In talking with some savvier real estate agents, they decided on how some of the high selling prices were brought.

In many cases, they are in poorly stocked areas, homes are listed well below the market, buyers come in, and hundreds of thousands of dollars exceed others. Yes, it is a comp, but it is also a unique buyer. This is often the case in Silicon Valley, where I flip, making underwriting difficult.

This means that it is important to see a potential "pop" flip story. Was it listed at $ 775,000, put on hold in 2 weeks, and then sold for $ 800,000? In my opinion, this is a significantly better comp than the home originally listed at $ 600,000.

Again, if you sell two homes in the $ 700,000 range, the transaction will look very good and may help raise the "comfortable underground selling price."

## NEAR THE MEDIAN PRICE OF A CITY OR REGION

Are you going to build the nicest and biggest house I've ever seen in this neighborhood?! If so, at least in my opinion, you are more likely to lose money.

How many people can afford the absolutely nice and most expensive homes in the area? a little. What if they are not in the new home market or just don't want to overuse them? Your flip can sit down.

It feels like a broken recorder, but this is not a big problem when the market is rising as it is now. However, problems can arise when things cool down.

The solution is to target properties that are resold at prices close to the median price of the city or region. How many buyers are there in the pool?

The point is to aim for a market segment with a large pool of buyers. If your home is really great, you probably have a little bit of a bidding war.

## CLEAR THE ADDED VALUE STORY

The first question to ask an agent when sending a flip to the agent is "What is the story of the house?" To be honest, what I am really looking for is a sign of pain. "The house was inherited, but no one had lived there for several years, and there was big damage to the roof.

They needed cash and were going to sell immediately." It's a good story because it shows you how to add value and why a house is sold at a discounted price.

Most importantly, you want to know how to add value to a property to make money with flips. It may be the ability to close quickly in cash, intensive refurbishment, or add-on / rebuild scenarios. All of these options have barriers that prevent entry and explain why you can trade beyond them.

It is cautious about buying a house that seems to steal at a good price. Don't get me wrong. I'm sure it's okay to buy a house at a great price, but I want to streamline why I'm doing a good deal.

With the spread of real estate technology, most people should be thinking about what their home is worth (perhaps even an inflated idea). I feel more comfortable buying a house if I can explain to myself why I can make a profit.

## NORMAL LAYOUT

This is one of the most overlooked aspects of a potential flipper house. The layout is important. I work with many homes built in the 1950s with strange additions. The saying approach of "pig lipstick" can be a loser.

Even more embarrassing is that there is no easy fix for Winchester Mansion. A leaky roof house is bad, but at least there is a reasonable price to fix it. A house with a bad layout is, of course, irreversible unless you break the whole house.

I understand that the term "normal layout" is subjective and a little vague. The test you use when walking around the house is to see if you can imagine the floor plan. It's relatively easy, but the layout feels fine. Another trick to use is to take women for every gentleman there because they understand these things better than most men.

## NICE SURROUNDING HOUSING

Are you buying the best house on the block or is it the worst? Other nearby houses do not need to be rebuilt, but a little ownership makes a big difference. More importantly, stay away from homes that look terrible or have problematic owners.

Walk around the neighborhood at different times of the day and talk to people outside. It may be a little awkward, but be honest, tell me what you are doing now. Most people are willing to share the dirt in their neighborhood.

## WHAT IS THE 70 PERCENT RULE

The 70 percent rule states that an investor should pay 70 percent of the ARV of a property minus the repairs needed. The ARV is the after repaired value and is what a home is worth after it is fully repaired.

# CHAPTER FIVE
# HOW TO FIND DEALS

Finding a house to flip involves two parts: selecting a market and searching for a specific property. Let's look at these one at a time.

## SELECT DOMESTIC MARKET

When figuring out how to find a reversing house, you need to decide which housing market you want to focus on before you start the process of finding a particular property. If you are just getting started, the answer is often simple: your own backyard.

Unless you are an experienced flipper trying to expand your business, you don't need to look further than your own market to find a home that flips simple and profitable for you.

Reversing in your own geographic market has several advantages. First of all, you know the region. You know what part of the town is more or less popular and you can feel the culture and charm of different regions.

This means that there is a better idea about the potential value of the house, beyond what is on paper (list of prices, specifications, comps, etc.).

Second, being physically close to the actual project itself saves time and money. You can visit the facility regularly before purchase or during the rehabilitation project itself. You may meet with a contractor and review several contractor teams before accepting a bid.

Like a job interview, meeting with a general contractor team is a great way to pick up intangible assets such as expertise that can be lost over the phone. If you need to travel a long distance to and from the site to perform these tasks, you can experience major headaches and stress.

Also, being close to property means that you can show the house when you sell the property, rather than hiring a third party. Please note that all third parties involved in the project have additional costs that reduce the margin. The more you can do yourself, the better.

The housing market is also defined by the type of housing. If you have limited reversal experience, you should focus on the most liquid products on the market. This is often a detached house with a median home price.

Think of it as a classic 3 bed, 2 bath house, not too flashy. The high buy / sell ratio of these properties with cash or funds from both homeowners and investors maximizes the exit strategy. These real estate's require less capital than high-end homes in the market, so there is less money risk.

Finally, we will focus on homes that require moderate renovation rather than larger homes. Scoping large projects requires a team of contractors with skills, experience, and trust. Therefore, do not overdo it until the belt is turned over several times.

## FIND A PROPERTY

Once you have identified your target market, there are various trading sources that you can consider to find a home that you can flip.

It is important to recognize that trading conditions can change depending on market conditions. For example, if house prices are low, auctions tend to be a good place to find a reversing house, but higher house prices may make the seller more profitable. The above sources are listed based mostly on the possibilities associated with rising home prices.

## AUCTION

In distressed markets, auctions are a great way to find low-priced properties that need rehabilitation. Houses sold at auction are seized and sold at discounted prices by lenders to minimize balance sheet losses. These steep discounts provide investors with large arbitrage opportunities, and competition is often limited because housing is not listed on the general market.

However, there are drawbacks. When dealing with foreclosure auctions, you will often encounter property liens that you will take over at the time of purchase. When purchasing a house at an auction, make sure that the title company is conducting a survey to understand what is happening and to get title insurance in case of an emergency.

Auctions often require the purchase of real estate completely on the spot. If the auction is a court step, you must have cash or cashier check on hand to win a bid and make a purchase. If the auction is online, other options may be available. Generally speaking, real estate must be purchased entirely in cash, which makes funding difficult. However, you can refinance after purchase and withdraw most of the assets from the assets.

## LEARN ABOUT AVERAGE MARKET PRICES.

The first step in finding a home to flip is to know the market. You need to understand the average price of the area you are looking for so that you can best identify the undervalued home.

Look at the various houses currently on the market to get an average price. This not only tells you which houses are undervalued but also gives you a sense of how many repaired houses you should sell.

You also need to investigate factors that affect the value of the house. Is the house in a safe area? Is it near a school or business district? Does it have factors that make it desirable for the average buyer? You will want to target underrated homes in these areas as you are more likely to sell them for a profit later.

## REO

If a foreclosure home does not sell at an auction, the bank or lender owns it. These homes are called real estate ownership (REO) lists. Given that the bank does not buy and sell houses, most people will want to remove these assets from the balance sheet and will sell them at a reasonable discount.

Some lenders send a list of REO properties by email or newsletter, but investors can simply call their local bank to ask if they are going to remove the property. As noted above, be aware of lien and fundamental damage to property before purchasing.

## SHORT SALE

If the homeowner defaults on a mortgage, the bank can choose to sell the house "short" or sell the property at a price less than the amount paid for the mortgage. Banks may prefer mortgages given that they must undertake to sell time-consuming and expensive processes (such as auctions and REOs) rather than mortgages.

If a bank approves a short sale of a house, this provides a good opportunity for buyers to get real estate at a discount.

There are several drawbacks to buying a short-sale property. Since lenders must approve short-term sales and sales prices, the sales process may take longer than traditional retail sales to complete.

In addition, the lenders who approve rarely agree to pay additional fees normally agreed to by the normal seller. This means that the cost of closing a buyer can be high.

However, like other sources, you can find houses that switch short sales, so don't exclude them. Ask the real estate agent about the short sale list and look for phrases such as "subject to bank approval," "before foreclosure," "requires review by the third party," "pre-authorization by bank." It is sold short.

## CONVENTIONAL (MLS)

The most traditional way to find (and list) home for sale is to use the Multiple Listing Service (MLS). MLS is a service that allows sellers to post lists to many different aggregators and websites to find homes across the Internet, allowing buyers to quickly and efficiently search thousands of real estate agent lists. If the house is for sale, it may be listed in the MLS.

The main drawback of finding a house that flips MLS is the high level of competition you face as a buyer. Given the thousands of people who use this service, it is difficult to find a property that presents a truly unique opportunity because homes priced under market prices are snapped up very quickly.

You must be a real estate agent to access MLS. That means you need to join a local real estate agent association. These associations require a fee of about $ 1,000 per year.

## SELLER DIRECT

If the price of a house is high and the market is relatively healthy, it is difficult to find a turning house. In fact, some of the best deals are not on the market because the seller has not yet decided to sell.

Seller direct (sometimes called direct sales) means that the homeowner is approaching a strategic time when the house has not yet been listed and is making an offer at an off-market home.

Before turning over and buying a house, do your homework on all these sources and feel what each offers. Again, there is no best or worst place to find a house to flip.

## WORKING WITH POTENTIAL PROPERTY LAWYERS

Partner with a probate lawyer. These lawyers work with family members who settle the assets (houses, cars, stocks, bonds, etc.) through the will-verification process and distribute them to the surviving heirs.

Knowing a will probate attorney can open up a wealth of opportunities, as there is virtually no competition in acquiring the property. In most cases, the family just wants to liquidate the asset from the property as soon as possible to receive the inheritance.

In this situation, there are very ambitious sellers. If you can close it quickly, you can usually use their desire to sell quickly for your benefit by buying real estate at a discounted price. It is also helpful to consult a lawyer.

**Alliance with a divorce lawyer:** As you can imagine, people tend to be a bit unreasonable and mean in the typical divorce process. Sometimes, some people tend not to care about what they receive as long as they receive even less. There are often homes for sale as a result of divorce.

**Partnership with bankruptcy lawyer:** These lawyers have clients who are applying for bankruptcy and may be interested in selling their homes before or after the application. Unfortunately for bankruptcy applicants, this type of attorney lead can be very lucrative.

You can also find bankruptcy sales notices in local newspapers because you need to post a notice before bankruptcy sales.

**Alliance with real estate lawyer**: In addition to handling property closures, this type of lawyer solves the problems people face in partnerships, cooperatives, joint ventures, and so on. I also know about real estate transactions that do not close for various reasons. And you can immediately make an offer to the seller.

# HOW TO MARKET FLIPPED HOUSES

## DIRECT MARKETING

### BANDIT SIGN

Use cheap bandit signs to promote your real estate investment business. These signatures can often be printed for $ 7-20 and attract an unlimited amount of prospects.

Paste them into the yard of all the properties you own or work on and place them at the intersection to attract sellers who will inevitably have to take down their property.

### DOOR HANGER

Door hangers are very cheap but very effective. If the prospect wants to go in and out of the house, they need to remove them so that your message is in their hands every time.

These can be placed in the rental community to attract home buyers for the first time, or to the homes of people who have fallen to default on mortgages.

In addition, using both sides of the door hanger and promoting other related services to each other, sponsors and strategic partners can select tabs and get free marketing for the real estate investment business.

## BULK SMS MARKETING

Mass SMS marketing is very cost-effective and versatile to find ambitious sellers and get them home quickly. You need to send a large number of text messages to the owner's list of potential customers for sale and announce new offers that will be sold to the buyer's network.

Unlike direct mail and telemarketing, almost 100% of text messages are read, and the action rate is high, resulting in incoming calls from people who want to do business. In addition, it costs only a few cents per piece compared to other marketing formats tested in the real estate investment business.

## INTERNET MARKETING

House flipping using internet marketing

Marketing is the lifeline of your business. "Marketing" is the process of acquiring potential customers and selling their homes. How do you make money correctly? And I will say that there are three main objectives related to its commercialization:

- Find motivated sellers
- Find cash buyer / investor or the retail buyer (create buyer list)
- Marketing to sell a house

Here is a list of the most common Internet marketing strategies for house flipping investment:

**Issuing Craigslist ads**: "We buy a home" (for motivated sellers) or "House with big discounts for sale" (for buyers / investors). Post here also to sell your home. And it's free!

**Website for sellers**: Create a business website. You can find motivated sellers by preparing multiple items such as "WE BUY

HOUSES." Have a way to capture your information to track your phone number and / or.

**Website for buyers**: This site needs to attract buyers and investors in cash and collect that information. You can also publish properties for sale here.

**SEO**: Another layer of website strategy is SEO (search engine optimization). There are free and paid ways for your website to have a higher ranking on Google.

**Free**: Keywords related to the entire site (real estate investment, home wholesale, home purchase, home cash, home cash payment, home discount for sale, etc.).

**Link websites to other websites**: article directories, social networks.

**Paid:** Pay Google to rank the highest site, Google Adwords. You pay to rank your keywords. Very competitive in the real estate investment field: it is a bidding system. The keyword "we buy a home" is more expensive to get a rating than "we buy a toilet." It can be expensive, but ROI can cover it.

You can also pay a marketing company to update SEO, post links, post on social networks, create articles, create videos for yourself, and more.

**Social network**: Create a Facebook page, YouTube page, Google+ page, LinkedIn profile. Post updates on these pages.

PLEASE POST A LINK TO YOUR WEBSITE.

Post on social media pages looking for a home to buy and make sure everyone knows. Create groups on Facebook and LinkedIn to build a network. Publish properties and share ideas, tips, and tricks.

## WHOLESALERS

Wholesalers: Finding the right investors for wholesale is very difficult. Generally, new real estate investors choose this niche to start an investment career. Therefore, most wholesalers you speak will probably never complete a deal in life.

Ninety-five percent of these wholesalers do not trade, do not know what a good deal is, or have never made a deal — Roger that. Now if you find a good wholesaler (only one) that can provide a useful sales opportunity for all the parties involved, you have found gold.

This is what you need to connect with them.

GO TO CRAIG LIST

Search for a house to buy

Call each of these people and ask if they are wholesalers.

Tell them that you are unfamiliar with real estate, you are very serious and have the funds to buy investment real estate.

Ask if there is a contracted real estate or potential business. Get contact information and save to CRM.

Call all signs (bandit signs) that appear locally and indicate that you want to buy a house, 95% of these people are wholesalers who may have a contract with you (follow the same tone for craigslist ads)

Now if your region looks like my region, you should probably have contacted 30-50 potential wholesalers that might give you the first deal.

## CHAPTER SIX
## THE FLIP FORMULAR

K nowing how to evaluate a contract is the key to success in this business! However, there are very few industries (investors, realtors, appraisers, etc.) that actually dominate this valuable skill.

You can "find" all the homes in the world, but unless you know how to properly evaluate them and make suggestions that will help you profit from House Flipping, you won't be useful.

In fact, many problems can arise if you do not know how to evaluate and provide properties properly.

Unfortunately, watching one of your home TV shows doesn't tell you how. In fact, many of the costs that can be very time consuming if not taken into account in the initial analysis of assets are omitted.

By understanding this principle, a "speculator," that is, a person who just buys a house in the hope of increasing its value is a true "investor," that is, a cost related to real estate rather than just speculation. You can become an understanding person. A true investor about the future knows exactly how to take a very calculated and accurate "risk" and generate a significant return on investment.

The four most important steps you need to understand to create an offer that almost always guarantees profitable transactions!

## DETERMINE ARV (VALUE AFTER REPAIR)

ARV is an acronym commonly used among real estate investors. This means "value after repair," basically the property is valuable after repair and update is complete. Once rehabilitation is complete, determining the amount of money worth the asset is always the first step in the process of evaluating the contract.

Knowing how much people pay for your property, you can determine all the other costs and determine the best place to get the right profit. If you don't know the ARV, there is no place to work.

ARV can be thought of as the final image of the puzzle. Once you know the appearance of the puzzle, you can place the pieces in the right place to create a profit image. Otherwise, you can spend time and energy to end what you don't want to see!

To accurately determine the ARV, you need to check Comparables or "Comps." Comps are recently sold homes (or homes for sale) similar to the property in question in the same general area. These are used to determine the "current rate" of a home in the area and are a very good indicator of what your home is sold for.

To access comparable property data, you can use paid or free services such as Zillow or Redfin, but to get the most detailed information in practice, the Multiple Listing Service, a service that provides almost everything. Or you need access to MLS details about the property for sale or recently sold.

To access MLS, you must work with an agent, become an agent yourself, or work with someone who has access to MLS.

The first step in MLS is to look for a "standard" rehabilitated sold composition that resembles the home condition when completed. These compositions are very easy to detect. They have improvements, good photos and shine over other homes. These compilations must be considered when determining ARV.

Then, depending on the number of "standard" sales compositions found, you can also consider other recently sold compositions such as short-selling or bank-owned properties (REOs) that have been updated or in good condition The .

As a rule, look for a house with the following criteria:

- Sold in the last 90-120 days.
- They are within ½ mile to 3/4 mile of your eligible property
- They are close in size, square feet, number of beds / baths, and age.
- They are in a similar neighborhood.

After reviewing recently sold compilations, you can expand your search results to the listed compilations (on sale) or pending (not yet closed under a buyer agreement).

The listed properties inform your competitors, so if you look at a rehabilitated house that isn't sold, you won't want to cherish the house more than what is listed.

With pending properties, you can see the future value, but be aware that it may not be sold at the set price.

Shortlists or pending sales (homes that sell at lower prices than the owner bears the lender) are rarely considered. This is a number launched by an agent to get a real estate offer. In many cases, the bank has not even performed an asset analysis, and there is a good chance that the short seller will never approve the sale of the property at the specified price.

I want to focus mainly on the modified properties, but also pay attention to properties that are similar to the property in question. If there are some comparable properties that are listed at a price lower than the recently sold or calculated offer, this may indicate that you are overpaid and the offer accordingly Can be reduced.

You may also want to check your tax records to see how much other investors have paid for homes purchased in the area.

Do not use works in another city, school district, or on the other side of a major barrier such as a highway, river, or railroad track. You can also take into account pools, garage sizes, lot sizes, views, and other updates, and adjust the values accordingly.

Finally, taking into account current market trends and seasonal price changes, you can indicate the resale price of real estate and the best time to buy and sell.

**EXAMPLE ONE**

If you find three standard rehabilitation homes that have been sold within the last two months and have the exact same floor plan as the property. They sold for $ 160,000, $ 155,000, and $ 150,000.

The one sold for $ 150,000 didn't have a granite countertop, but the other two were yours when the rehabilitation ended. And you also see only one rehabilitated property listed for 5 days and currently pending $ 160,000. You will see that the one rehabilitated property that is only on the market for two days and is listed for $ 160,000.

The property has an ARV of at least $ 155,000, and you can be confident that ARV is $ 157,500 when calculating your own offer.

**EXAMPLE TWO**

Last month we found one rehabilitated standard sale that sold for $ 120,000. The two recently sold REOs are also displayed. One has a new carpet and paint, which sold for $ 100,000. The other is not as beautiful as the standard sales, but it looks better than the other REOs and sells for $ 110,000.

You can also see the standard sale pending for $ 125,000 and the sale listed for $ 130,000. I don't want to use a value of $ 130,000 or $ 125,000 because I don't know if these properties will actually sell at that price, but this additional data support the values found in standard sales and is confident at $ 120,000 can be used as an ARV when determining offers.

The value can be easily determined, or it can be a little difficult. If in doubt, always be careful when making an offer!

**ESTIMATE REPAIR COSTS**

The next step in accurately determining the offer price is to estimate the cost of repair. In my company, this has become so good that you can easily see the photos or get someone's description, and if you know the age and size of the house, within 1-2% without looking. You can guess the repair costs at home is never home!

The "$ 20 per square foot" rule is a guide used to get a pretty good idea about the cost of home repairs. Simply put, this rule comes from our experience that most homes that require full "standard" beauty rehabilitation cost about $ 20 per square foot.

It may not be"standard" beauty rehabilitation

"Standard" cosmetic rehabilitation usually includes all new floors (carpet and hard surface floors), paint (interior and exterior), baseboards, electrical and plumbing fixtures, new kitchen / bathroom (cabinet, granite) Include electrical appliances), include blinds and windows, doors, and possibly a little landscaping.

For example, if you buy a house of about 1,500 square feet, you can plan to spend about $ 30,000 for rehabilitation (1,500 x $ 20 = $ 30,000).

Currently, this rule assumes that you are rehabilitating an entrance or some type of intermediate entrance house. If you are rehabilitating a high-end home and using higher quality materials and finishes, adjust to a rate close to $ 25 or $ 30 per square foot. But for standard basic rehabilitation, the rule of $ 20 per square foot is optimal.

From this point, you can adjust it up or down according to your additional needs (or unnecessary ones). For example, if you need to rebuild the roof, you need to add $ 5,000 to $ 8,000. New HVAC? Probably about $ 5,000. A new pool or resurfacing team will provide an additional $ 5,000. And new windows cost about $ 200 per window.

You will also need to add additional costs if you are redistributing electricity, plumbing, or doing something structural in your home.

Now, on its "inversion" side, you can adjust the price estimate if you don't have to do some standard items.

For example, if you already have a newly renovated kitchen in your house, you can eliminate it from rehabilitation costs. In fact, if you only need to repaint the interior and replace the carpet and other small items, you can make the whole house for just $ 2,000-

$ 5,000. It depends only on what the house needs to bring it to sale value (or after repair).

Over time, you will have a better understanding of these costs and can easily calculate the cost of rehabilitation. We will discuss rehabilitation and work with contractors to explore this issue in more detail in future publications.

It is important to remember that you will probably only use this $ 20 formula per square foot when getting the initial offer price. Once you get an "approval" for the offer, you'll probably look at the property with an authorized contractor to get a more detailed "work area" and repair quote, so you don't miss anything important

You can do it yourself, or you can contact them if you are considering "wholesale" the property to another investor.

## CALCULATE EXPENSE CLOSE AND HOLD

This is one area that seems to "forget" to mention these entire house flipping shows. I don't know if they think it's "sexy" to show greater profits, but flipping the house sucks all the money you thought you earned into the cost of closure and retention If you find out, it's not so exciting.

Below are some of the holding and completion costs that you need to know when calculating investment property offers.

### PURCHASE COMPLETION COST

These are the closing costs incurred when buying a home. Traditionally, most of the commission and closing costs are paid by the seller, so the cost of buying a property is usually less than when selling the property.

This is about transaction analysis, and my goal is not to explain all the costs associated with buying a house, so for now buy when buying a house to buy closing costs Just calculate 0.5% of the price.

**COST OF SALE**

This is a place that can be a bit more expensive. If you sell a house with an agent, you can usually rely on a 5-6% fee for the agent. Depending on the region and market, the buyer may ask for a concession that helps pay for the cost. This ranges from 1-6% but is usually about 3%.

Next, include about 1% in additional closing costs such as title and escrow or attorney fees.

So if you use an agent to sell a house, selling the closing costs may actually increase. And your buyer is asking for a concession. Depending on the area and type of house we are dealing with, it usually accounts for 6% to 10% of the selling price of closing costs.

**HOLDING COST**

More often than closing costs are usually costs that many people forget to take into account when buying an investment property. Cost of ownership includes property tax, insurance, utilities, lawn maintenance, HOA, and Mello-Roos (if any).

You'll need to see what these costs are, and check how long you 'll retain the properties for which you 'll need to calculate these costs during this period.

## FUNDING COSTS

If you're using capital, you don't have to worry about funding costs but consider this if you need to use funding as you would someone else.

If you have a private money lender, you can pay an 8-12% return on capital annually. If you are using a hard money lender in the current market, you can expect to pay about 12% per year, plus additional points and fees. (Points are simply a flashy way to represent percentage points.)

Most hard money lenders charge 2-3 points (basically 2-3%), but this is not annualized, so regardless of how long you borrow money, this is what you pay for the borrowed money is. Fees vary, but you can calculate additional "points" or an additional 1% for these costs.

Therefore, for funding, if you pay 12% private lenders annually, it will be the same as 1% each month you borrow money. If you plan to hold the property for 4 months, you need to calculate 4% of the borrowed capital. If you are using hard money, you need to calculate an additional 2-3%, so the funding cost for 4 months will be about 3-7%.

For example, if you borrow $ 100,000 from a private render, you borrow money that pays 1% or $ 1,000 each month. If you own for 4 months, you will pay $ 4,000.

Or, as another example, if you borrow the same $ 100,000 to a gold lender, calculate about 2-3% immediately from the door. This is $ 2,000-3,000. Then every month you owe money to pay an additional 1% or $ 1,000. So, from the previous example, you will pay $ 6,000-7,000 for funding costs for 4 months.

We will continue to investigate this, and you will hear it more and understand it as you begin to practice it. Eventually it will all become second nature! We'll talk more about funding costs later, but make sure you're calculating for this because you can actually add up!

## CALCULATE THE PROFIT

Profit is your ultimate goal. It is a reward for your deterioration, sleepless nights, risk, and diligence. You need to make sure that you are reasonably safe and compensated. On average, homes are sold at about 92% of their original list price.

This means that if you think you will sell your home for $ 100,000, you are very likely to get only $ 92,000. So in this scenario, if you build with an expected profit margin of $ 5,000, you're all done and lose $ 3,000.

It is usually taken at a profit margin of about 15% compared to the expected final selling price. I never fall below 10 percent. There are too many questions. In almost every transaction, refurbishment costs are higher than expected, and in most cases, homes are sold cheaper than expected.

In this business, you have to move your home fast. That often means you have to leave a little profit. You can't sit home for another three months to wait for the buyer's willingness to pay the top dollar, not when you pay the private capital rate and miss other opportunities.

## OFFER DETERMINATION

### FORMULA 1

(ARV)-(Repair costs)-(closure and maintenance costs)-(desired benefits) = offer price

It's very easy. This is the most basic and obvious formula and is probably the most accurate way to determine the price of an offer.

Basically, you will find a reason to sell a house and deduct all the costs and benefits you want. And it gives you the price of your offer. ☺

Of course, the profit you want depends on you and how much you want to earn. I want to be conservative and leave room for error, but if the offer is too low, you will soon find it very unlikely to buy many homes.

In most cases, it is recommended that profits be based on a% rather than standard numbers. In the coming weeks to months, you will understand why I say this more, but it is related to risk management, return on capital, and a broader perspective when assembling parts of your home dump machine

Well, again, I am moving forward. As a first simple rule, you can calculate 10% of ARV for profit. So if ARV is $ 250,000, you can calculate a profit of $ 25,000.

An example is as follows: A 2,000 square foot house has a $ 220,000 ARV, which requires standard rehabilitation and a new HVAC, funding everything through a private lender. According to those numbers, I:

ARV = $ 220,000

Repair cost = ($ 20 / square foot x 2,000 square feet =) $ 40,000 + (new HVAC =) $ 5,000 = $ 45,000

Closing and retention costs = 1% (purchasing closing) + 8% (closed sales) + $ X (retention) + 1% / month (private money finance) = about $ 18,000

Desired profit = $ 22,000 (10% of ARV)

Or $ 220,000-85,000 ($ 45,000 + $ 18,000 + $ 22,000) = $ 135,000 offer price.

This makes the calculation of investment property offers faster and easier. You can hear this formula called "70% rule". Here it is .

Formula # 2

ARV x 70%-Repair cost = offer price

Basically, take what to sell when the property is modified, subtract the cost of the modification, then leave 30% to cover the closure and holding costs, and the desired profit.

Here is an example

If the fixed or retail price (ARV) is $ 200,000, and it costs $ 25,000 to repair a home to reach retail conditions, this is how the offer is calculated.

$ 200,000 (ARV) x 70%-$ 25,000 (repair) = $ 115,000

It's very easy.

I want to be very clear here. This is not a single formula for everyone, but it should be adjusted according to the scope of the project you are working on, the time required, the type of funds you want to earn, the acquisition strategy, and the current market conditions. Your offer

Note that this same formula is used between 60% and 80% (or even 90%). But if you are just getting started, adjusting from there using the 70% rule can be very "safe."

## ESTIMATING REHAB COST

### HOW TO ESTIMATE REHABILITATION COSTS

Simply put, experience, time, and practice are required. Get out there and see as many properties as you can find. Use your camera phone to carefully shoot the property state and return to this list to create a rough estimate.

The following construction items and systems are not a complete list but should give a pretty good idea of what to expect when estimating the cost of rehabilitating a house.

Again, pricing these components is highly dependent on the local market. Material pricing is subject to local taxes.

Therefore, the pricing described in this guide below is a very rough average and should only be used as a starting point and considered as a way to assess the competitiveness of a contractor's bid.

Note: Rehabilitation costs vary greatly by state and city, as described above, and can actually cause frustration for new investors.

This online rehabilitation quote calculator uses regularly updated data from one of the oldest and most respected constructions cost book companies. They provide nationwide construction costs indexed by zip code. You can select items and quantities, add them to the list, and use them to compare contractor bids.

Let's go to some details of the rehabilitation cost considerations for each of these homes, starting with the demo and taking away the material.

## DEMOLITION AND HAULING

Demolition costs vary greatly depending on the type of material being removed. Usually, the harder to delete, the heavier it is, the more expensive it is. For example, the cost of removing a tacked carpet is only $ 1.40 per SY for a crew, while removing a glued hardwood can cost as much as $ 25 per SY.

HAULING

Transportation costs are divided into transportation costs and disposal costs. For transportation, you can start with $ 230 + $ 50 / ton for a 40CY bottle, and you can expect dump disposal fees to be around $ 75 / ton.

When estimating transportation and disposal costs, the weight of the waste makes a big difference. For example, the weight of 1CY wood waste is about 0.25 tons, but the weight of 1CY concrete is about 1.25 tons, which is five times higher. Depending on the degree of dismantling, the 1000 SF house will need to take the bottle up to 5 times.

Demonstration and transportation of a complete building with remaining structures do not include transportation costs but can be paid approximately $ 5 per SF without disposal costs.

Next, let's look at the material and cost of items outside the property.

## OUTSIDE

## SIDING & TRIM

Many old houses have wooden sidings called clapboards. It can be fixed with wood filler and painted or replaced about every 10 years. Other forms of siding include aluminum, asbestos, vinyl, and stucco. Aluminum siding is more fragile, harder to repair, and more difficult to paint than wooden siding.

Asbestos siding is usually not dangerous and generally hard to break, and can easily be painted or covered with another type of siding, but this may not be desirable due to the disclosure law. Vinyl siding lasted a long time and did not require painting, so it almost replaced another siding.

Estimating siding replacement costs: When measuring siding, measure the area of the wall to be repaired or replaced, ignoring wall openings. Depending on the quality of the siding, the installation of a normal vinyl siding will cost $ 340-650 / CSF of wall area. CSF refers to 100 square feet.

## PAINT

There are many considerations when painting the exterior of a house, such as the surface to be painted and the height of the building. Before doing so, you should consider whether you need to paint and whether you can achieve the same effect with a simple power wash.

Estimating painting costs: The typical cost of repainting a house exterior with 1 coat of paint with 2 painting hours and 1 gallon of paint per 100 SF (1 CSF) is about $ 160 / CSF or $ 1.60 / SF . Next, you need to add height cost and trim paint.

For example, if the height is between 8 feet and 13 feet, the cost increases by 30%. If the height is between 13 and 17 feet, the painting cost can be increased by 60%.

WINDOW AND DOOR

WINDOW

Replacing the window can increase the resale value of the property, but can be quite expensive if you cannot find a stock window with standard measurements.

For example, if the window opening matches a standard vinyl window, you can pay between $ 275 and $ 400, depending on the size of the opening and the glazing options. On the other hand, creating a custom vinyl window to fit a non-standard opening doubles the price.

DOOR

Exterior door prices range from $ 200 for basic slab doors to $ 2,000 for stylish oak or mahogany entrances. You can pay about $ 1,500 to cut a wall opening and install a slab door.

Interior doors are much cheaper and usually range from $ 100 to $ 500 depending on the material, style, and size.

KITCHEN CABINET

There are many options for improving kitchen cabinets, from laundry to painting, surface finishing, and replacement.

**Thumb estimation rules**

When replacing cabinets, there is a simple rule of thumb for estimating the space in a home cabinet and counter. The figure shows the square feet on the counter or cabinet surface per 1000 square feet of living area floor (all under the roof except the garage, roof, patio, and porch).

Reserve a little more counter and cabinet space in a small house (less than 1,200 square feet) Less space are required for a very large house (over 4,000 square feet). Measure the square foot of the counter, whichever is shorter, either the front end or the rear end

Base cabinet: 7 linear feet per 1,000 square feet of living area

Wall cabinet: 6 linear feet per 1,000 square feet of living area

Drawer base cabinet: 1 per 10 linear feet of base cabinet

**Cost considerations**

A cabinet is like a furniture. Prices vary greatly. For example, drawers with hardwood rails, plywood bottoms, and dovetails are considerably more expensive than stapled butted particleboard drawers.

High-quality custom and semi-custom cabinets are 3/4 "or 1/2" furniture grade plywood covered with a hardwood veneer. The drawer has fully extended roller hardware. Inexpensive cabinets are usually made of 3/8 inch or 1/2 inch particleboard with a mel-amine coating.

"Ready to assemble" cabinets are the cheapest and are sold mainly in do-it-yourself stores. Options are limited, and it takes about an hour for the unit to be ready for installation.

COUNTERTOP

Thumb estimation rules

The rule of thumb for estimating the needs of a home countertop is as follows:

Counter: 8 linear feet per 1,000 square feet of living area

Counter width and height: 25 inches wide x 36 inches high

**Cost**

Similar to cabinets, countertops come in a variety of materials, ranging from laminates that start at about $ 30 / LF to a variety of stones that cost over $ 100 / SF.

OTHER CONSIDERATIONS

Extensive kitchen modifications usually require HVAC work such as moving ducts, registers, grills, hot water pipes, or radiators. Consider the cost of patching walls or ceilings after moving or adding HVAC material. Assume half a day ($ 150) work as the minimum charge for drywall hanging, taping and finishing.

BATHROOM

There are two types of bathroom jobs. The first method makes better use of available space. The second is to add space by expanding existing bathrooms or adding entirely new bathrooms. Both types are expensive when calculated based on the cost per square foot of floor.

A proper bathroom plan will minimize plumbing and electrical wiring and place plumbing fixtures on one wall. This arrangement allows fixtures to share a common waste line and roof vent.

Construction costs associated with bathroom refurbishment include waste lines, service lines, installation of electricity, installation of bathtubs and showers, supporting joists under the bathtub, installation of vanity, toilets, floor and wall tiling Work included.

## Cost

The cost of installing a standard enameled steel bathtub without connection is between $ 215 and $ 360. Installed bathtub wall kits can run for $ 250-750 installed. Installing a faucet can cost well over $ 110 to $ 1000 depending on the equipment used.

For a basic white toilet, toilet settings start at $ 120. The installation of the pedestal washroom starts at $ 120 for the basic model and can exceed thousands if replaced with a furniture quality cabinet and stone counter and sink.

The cost of tiling is similar to flooring tiling and again depends heavily on the materials used.

PLUMBING

Plumbing and HVAC contractors usually do not list materials and labor costs separately, but only estimate the total installation price, so there is no good average data on this. There are some fairly common jobs.

SERVICE UPGRADE

Upgrades to galvanized water pipes with copper pipes include fittings and pipe clips using type M copper pipes with soft solder joints, and costs from $ 7 to $ 12 / LF.

SEWER

The drainage system consists of sewers, drains, and vents. Often old pipes are broken or clogged. Old houses have cast iron drains that rust after about 70 years. In some cases, the pipe diameter will be smaller than required by the current code. If pipes are visible when the cast iron is visible, the code will need to update the drain as well.

Removing cast iron drainpipe, waste and vent pipe (DWV) and replacing with ABS pipe with fittings and 4 inch ABS plastic pipe with solvent welded joint will cost $ 12- $ 22 / LF.

WATER HEATER

Gas water heater installation is also a common piping requirement. Gas water heater installation includes temperature and pressure relief valves and pipe connection work. Costs do not include the addition of flue, water pipes, gas pipes, fitting materials, and gas licensing fees as needed. Basic 30 gallon water heater

ROOFING

AVERAGE LIFE

The lifetime of the roof depends on the type of roof installed. A typical 3-tab single lasts about 20 years, an architectural single lasts 45 years, and a tile lasts up to 150 years. Often, part of the need for a new roof is the result of roof deck deterioration. In addition, the roof overlaid on the old roof shortens the average lifespan by 10-15 years.

MEASUREMENT

To measure a flat roof, divide the area into rectangles, calculate each area, and add up the total. To accurately calculate the roof surface of a sloped roof, the length of the rafters must be multiplied by the width of each pitch.

However, if the roof pitch is less than 5/12, a simple rule of thumb will give you almost the same result in a very short time.

Multiply the length and width of the building, including eaves and overhangs. Divide by 100 to find the number of "squares" on the roof. Next, add 10 percent to the gable roof, 15 percent to the hip roof, and 20 percent to the roof with the dormer. A square is equivalent to 100 square feet.

## Cost

Stripping the roof costs $ 50 per square dollar for asphalt to $ 100 per square dollar for tiles, but this cost does not cover transportation.

The new shingle roof starts at $ 230 / SQ for a basic 20-year shingle and nearly $ 400 / SQ for 40-year shingles with fire and wind resistance. Clay tiles start at nearly $ 800 / SQ, and red slate can run up to $ 3,600 / SQ.

DECK AND POOL

BASIC DECK

The standard pillar and beam wooden deck use pressure-treated framing wood with 4 "x 6" pillars set in concrete. Basic estimates include concrete, pressure-treated struts, beams, central 12-inch joists, unfinished deck boards, galvanized hardware, fasteners, 4 'wide staircase from deck level to ground level, In the center is a handrail 4 " height 36 'rail, stair rail.

## Cost

Using pressure-treated slabs, Edeck materials can go from SF $ 34 / SF up to $ 60 / SF.

POOL CONSIDERATIONS

Ground pools may need to be repainted approximately every 5 to 10 years, but this is expensive and rarely done by homeowners, so this maintenance may need to be done.

**Cost**

The cost of preparing a plasterer pool is approximately $ 20 per LF around the pool, and the cost of repainting the plasterer is approximately $ 60 per LF around the pool.

The inside of the properties described in the next section can be the most difficult due to a large number of hidden elements.

INTERNAL

PAINT

Painting the interior of a house is more expensive than the exterior. Because it takes about 30% of the time

Typical painting costs are per 100 square feet of the floor when painting with a roller and brush once on the walls and ceilings of all rooms in residence, including bathrooms and closets.

Costs for painting cabinets, trims, doors, and window trims are not included. This includes minimal surface treatment, sachets of minor defects in wallboard or plaster, masking of adjacent surfaces, and priming of stained or discolored surfaces.

**Cost**

Estimated painting costs: For 3 painter hours and 1-gallon paint per 100 square feet of floor, you will have to pay about $ 230.

DRYWALL, CEILING

To add drywall workforce, three coats of electrical boxes and cutting boards around obstacles, mounting on 8 'to 12' wall studs or ceiling joists on the floor, joint tape, joint compound Includes finish polishing. Material includes 38 feet premixed joint compound per 100 square feet, 38 linear feet

2-inch perforated joint tape per 100 square feet, 1/2 pound drywall screw per 100 square feet, 10% waste.

**Cost**

Estimating drywall costs: Typically, 3/8 inch boards are used for the ceiling and ½ inch for the walls. You should expect to pay about the US $ 2 / SF on the ceiling and about US $ 1.80 / SF on the wall.

NUMBER OF FLOORS

Some types of floor coverings are more durable than others. Vinyl lasts longer than carpet. Ceramic tiles last longer than wood blocks or strip flooring. All floor coverings require a structurally sound, clean, horizontal (1/4 inch per 10 feet) and dry base (no more than 13% moisture below the floor).

Assuming that the surface is smooth and has a good moisture barrier, concrete is a good foundation. Unconditioned hard boards, plywood, and particle boards are also good foundations for flooring. Use 1/4 inch or 3/8 inch thick sheets. The underlay requires a 1/32 inch gap between ends to allow expansion.

WOOD

If the wooden floor is smooth and free of large cracks, repairs may return the floor to a new state. Most wooden floors can be polished and refinished several times.

**Cost**

Floor polishing costs can start at $ 61 per CSF. Most of the flooring installation costs are included in the material, and you can expect to pay $ 3.50 for unfinished oak and over $ 15 for wide hardwood.

CERAMIC TILE

Ceramic tiles can be set in mortar (thin or thickset) or applied with adhesive. The cleanup will take some time, but the adhesive is more convenient because it does not need to be mixed.

The tiles are placed on a backboard, and cement board reinforced with glass mesh coated with the polymer.

**Cost**

Tile Cost Estimate: Setting up a tile with glue can start at over $ 7 per sci-fi without including the cost of the tile itself. Doing this with a thin-set can start over $ 14 / SF. The cost of the tile itself will also vary between styles and travertine prices between $ 1.50 and over $ 15.

CARPET

If the gap is filled and the surface is not loose, the carpet can be installed directly on an existing hardwood floor. Carpet installation includes prepared surface sweep, carpet tax trip settings, pad recombination, 12 to 15-foot wide carpet deployment, measurement, marking, cutting, trimming at one end, seam hot Includes disposal of melt tape and debris.

**Cost**

For standard quality carpets, you can expect to pay about $ 50 / SY.Air conditioner

FORCED AIR HEATING

A common update is to add heating and forced air cooling to an old house. The capacity of Btu's residential heating system depends on the weather, window size and direction, insulation, and the area to be heated.

Estimating needs

To estimate the cost, there is a simple way to calculate the required oven Btu capacity. Multiply the heated floor area by 53. Then round to the next larger oven size. For example, to set the size of a 2,000 square foot home oven:

2,000 x 53 is 106,000. The next largest oven size is 125,000 Btu.

The installation of the 125,000 Btu gas oven has a duct on the inner wall that contains a humidifier, filter, 5-8 galvanized sheet duct, resistor and grill, thermostat and electrical connection, gas line and pipe connection. Gas, ventilation, and ventilation chimney accessories, supply and return air chambers, system activation, and balance.

**Cost**

This costs $ 4,000 to $ 7,300, excluding the wall, floor, and ceiling patches as needed.

INSTALLATION OF AIR CONDITIONER

The installation of a 5-ton air conditioning unit added to an existing forced-air oven includes remote condensers and pads, coils and cabinets, cooling pipes, new thermostats, electrical wiring, and connections. This costs between $ 5,700 and $ 10,000.

ELECTRICAL

SERVICE UPDATE

Old house services are generally inadequate and may need to be updated to 200 amps. In addition, if the panels are made in the Federal Pacific, they will probably need to be replaced. The installation of a 200 Amp service cabinet will start at about $ 300.

## WIRED

Almost all new homes today are wired with a non-metal-clad cable called Romex, but that may not be what you will find when working in an old home. There are surprises depending on age.

## TYPE

Houses built before 1930 generally had knob and tube wiring (K & T). The cable was hung between a pole and a porcelain insulator placed on joists. When the wire needed to pass through the structure, a hollow porcelain tube was inserted into a stud or joist hole. The conductor was usually an individual wire covered with fabric insulation.

Aluminum wire is another type that is no longer used in household electrical systems. Aluminum is an excellent durable conductor and is generally less expensive than the most popular copper. In the 1970s, they discovered that aluminum wires are prone to arcing and fire at connections.

## SIZE

The size of the power cord is measured with a US wire gauge (AWG) and is usually abbreviated with a pound sign. For example, # 14-3 shows a 14 gauge wire (and possibly a separate bare ground wire) with three conductors.

The smaller the gauge number, the larger the cable and the greater the current capacity

Most circuits in the house have 15 amps of power and use 14 gauge copper wire, while kitchenware circuits have 20 amp capacity and should use 12 gauge copper wire. Electric water, air conditioner, or clothes dryer is 30 amps, 10 gauge copper wire must be used, and electric stove requires 6 gauge copper wire and

50 amp circuit breaker. All of these cables require a copper ground wire.

**Cost**

For exposed walls, the cost of a Romex 14 gauge is $ 1.40 to $ 4.00 / LF. Conduit diameters range from $ 1.50 to $ 8.00 / LF depending on the diameter.

Receptacle

In most rooms, the cord should not exceed 6 'along the floor line from the outlet. That is, there should be an exit every 12 inches along the wall.

Plan 6 dual outputs per 20 amp circuit. Electricians can suggest ways to insert 10 or 12 plugs into the circuit but still meet NEC requirements. Each room requires a switch-operated ceiling light or a switch-operated outlet. In this code, the switch must be placed next to the entrance door of the room.

**Cost**

Installation of a metal duct box, including switches, receptacles, top fixtures or ceiling fans, costs between $ 10 and $ 30 EA.

SMOKE DETECTOR

Almost all community codes require a minimal number and place-ment of smoke detectors, so you should plan to add them as needed.

Understanding how to accurately estimate rehabilitation costs is only possible if there is no emergency funding for unexpected re-pairs. This is where unexpected rehabilitation costs occur.

## CHAPTER SEVEN
## HOW TO CORRECTLY EVALUATE AND
## ANALYZE INVESTMENT PROPERTY

How to correctly evaluate and analyze investment property unlike stocks, there is no easy way to determine the exact value of the current or planned property. Enriching real estate means buying, maintaining and holding as long as possible to build wealth on real estate.

**PROPERTY EVALUATION**

It's all income. As a real estate investor, you need to identify what realistic income your target property can generate on a sustainable basis year by year. Current and historical revenue figures are the most important.

Once the revenue range is determined, you can calculate the property's total rental yield and price for revenue valuation and compare it to other properties in the neighborhood.

**PRICE INCREASES ARE SECONDARY**

One of the main reasons why the housing bubble has occurred and then collapsed is because investors have moved away from the income component of the property and focused on potential property valuations.

Investors didn't mind that cash flow was very negative if they could get on the wave within 1-2 years and make a profit.

When the party stopped, speculators were crushed, affecting Domino and hurting neighbors who planned to buy and hold. If you are mainly focused on property valuation, not income, you are a speculator. Real estate has no real value if you don't generate income or save rent.

## PROPERTY PRICES ARE CLOSELY RELATED TO INFLATION.

Real estate price increases generally track inflation by +/- 2%. In other words, if the latest inflation rate is 3%, domestic property prices can be expected to rise by 1-5%. Over the years, real estate price fluctuations can, of course, fluctuate significantly.

However, looking at real estate prices for 10 years, there is a relatively smooth correlation. It becomes a delusion when a consistent price increase of 10% per year is expected. Remember that rising property prices need to be considered as a secondary attribute. If that happens, it's great. If not, focus on cash flow.

## PROPERTIES ARE ALWAYS LOCAL

Be careful not to extrapolate property statistics. Just because there are reports that San Francisco property prices rose 19.6% in May over the previous year does not mean you can sell your house up 19.6%. The house price is probably 10% higher than the median. National statistics can be thrown out of the window as well.

The best price to know what your home is worth is whether your neighbor sells it. Real estate price statistics show the general direction and relative strength of prices.

## STEPS FOR EVALUATING PROPERTIES

**Calculate the annual total rent yield:** Get realistic monthly market rent based on the comparisons you can find online and multiply by 12 to get annual rent. Here, the total annual rent is obtained and divided by the market price of the property. Example: $ 2,000 / month = $ 24,000 / year. $ 24,000 / $ 500,000 = total rent yield 4.8%. The annual gross rental yield is to pay 100% cash and get a quick snapshot of what the potential of the blue sky looks like in real estate if there is no ongoing expense.

**Compare the total rent yield to the risk-free rate:** The risk-free rate is a 10-year bond yield. Investors say "no risk" because the US government has virtually zero chance of defaulting debt. All investments require a risk premium rather than a risk-free rate. If the total annual rent yield for the property is lower than the risk-free rate, dig deeper or move forward.

**Calculate the annual net rental yield (capitalization rate):** Net rental yield is basically net operating revenue divided by the market value of the real estate. Net operating income is calculated by subtracting mortgage rates, insurance, property taxes, HOA fees, marketing and maintenance costs from gross annual revenue. In other words, the actual annual profit is calculated. It can be added by depreciation, but this is not a cash expense, but it focuses on cash flow.

**Compare the net rental yield with the risk-free rate:** Ideally, the net rental yield should be above the risk-free rate. The principal is paid overtime. This increases the net profit of the rental and extends the risk-free rate. If everything goes well, your rent will rise, and your property will be appreciated.

**Calculate property price / return:** The P / E ratio is simply the market value of your property divided by the current net operating profit.

**Real estate price forecast and rental forecast:** P / E ratios and rental returns are instantaneous. The real opportunity is to anticipate expectations properly.

The best way to predict the future is to compare what has happened in the past with online graphics provided by DataQuick, Redfin, and Zillow and make realistic expectations about the growth of local employment.

Does the employer move to the city or retire? Does the city allow more land development, or are there restrictions such as building heights? Is the city in financial difficulties and trying to impose more property taxes on the owner?

## PROPERTY EVALUATION IS PART SCIENCE
## PART GUESSWORK

The more open houses you deal with from start to finish, the more you get used to the exercise of evaluating property values. It becomes the sixth sense to know immediately whether the property is a good deal.

If you want to get a feel for the local market, make sure to visit the open house weekly for months if you buy real estate.

High selling costs, mainly at 5-6% commission levels, cannot fully emphasize how real estate is considered a long-term investment. The reason why real estate agents do not want to reduce the rate to increase volume is completely confusing to me.

In mass production markets such as San Francisco, the volume is reduced by 40-50%. It is worth doing your own research and checking similar prices online.

Assets are tangible assets, unlike stocks that can lose value in nanoseconds for countless reasons. Mortgage payment? I encourage everyone to diversify their net assets into property and tangible assets such as what you can become a price setter.

# HOW TO NEGOTIATE WHEN BUYING A HOUSE

### DON'T LIMIT YOUR OPTIONS TO A FEW HOUSES

Please review your options closely so that you know the right home when you see it. Scouting neighborhoods and homes in advance

The better you understand the top priorities (price, house condition, location, size, school district, commuting?), the more you can combine and match those priorities when negotiating a particular home.

Place yourself in a flexible situation so that you can act quickly when the right house is on the market. When looking for a home for a growing family, the five fathers spent months opening the home and tracking sales prices.

When the right place appeared on the market, he immediately identified it, made a strong offer, and immediately got the house.

You need to have Plan B for any property, knowing what Plan B is, you can negotiate. If Plan B is significantly worse than the house you are considering, you suffer a negotiating penalty.

## DO NOT NEGOTIATE BASED ON THE ASKING PRICE

Negotiate based on the total cost of the transaction and the total cost of owning the house, and the reality is spotlighting two numbers, what the seller wants and what the buyer pays. However, they are not important figures

If a home is expensive to repair and maintain, getting a home at a price lower than the suggested price is considered a victory, but it can be a false win. For buyers, the first and most important number is the amount you need to pay to purchase the house, including fees, points (prepaid fees paid to lenders to lower mortgage interest rates), and closing costs. Another equally important number is that it takes months to own the house.

Sellers should focus on both the amount you earn after deducting sales commissions and commissions and the net assets you can earn after the sale, not the total selling price.

## DON'T NEGOTIATE ONLY ABOUT MONEY

Negotiate with an array of terms. All cash transactions often outperform other offers in TV show negotiations, but in practice, most buyers rely on mortgage lenders.

For example, you can emphasize intent by preventing more serious money from being refunded when a transaction survives an important stage such as assessment or home inspection.

This gives sellers an incentive to be patient with the lender process. Also, if you are a seller, don't rush the offer even if the first reaction to a low-priced offer is in. "Find the buyer's rationale. Perhaps they are looking at something in the market or home that you are not.

Using a long process of negotiations, understanding the other party's priorities and perspectives should facilitate negotiations as they approach the agreement.

## DO NOT PUT BUDGETS AND PRIORITIES ON ALL AGENTS YOU MEET

Contract with you and an agency that represents you only, It is especially important to have a buyer's agent (buyer) who is solely responsible for you. This is because price adjustments are made to offset defects and other complications found in home inspections.

In the initial negotiations, we were telling the listing agent that we would only treat it as a credit as a flaw. But it's not automatic, and if you have too many defects and credits, you might not want the house.

# CHAPTER EIGHT
# STEPS IN REHABBING PROPERTIES

The rehabilitation process can be divided into seven stages. The same is highly recommended in the rehabilitation business to help streamline the overall flipping process. Save time and money because it's important to have a proven system. Below is a quick list of the entire rehabilitation strategy.

**The work development scope**: Create a step-by-step checklist detailing exactly what the contractor should do throughout the facility.

**Recruitment and contractor selection:** Inform potential contractors that they are not retail customers when bringing multiple employees to bid on business.

**Communicating contracts with the company**: As an investor, it is important to protect yourself. Please sign the appropriate documents before starting rehabilitation.

**Important documents**: sign the following documents: independent contractor contract, scope of work, payment schedule, contractor insurance compensation form, W-9 tax form

**Managing the rehabilitation process**: In this phase, the contractor is managed through physical rehabilitation

**Facility closures**: Facility closures should include the final tour and final payment to the contractor.

**Prepare for sale**: Clean up your property as soon as possible and get ready for sale.

## REPAIRED PROPERTY TYPE

In many cases, there are several categories of specific property exit strategies, as do the rehabilitation. There are three main types of rehabilitation projects that investors should consider.

- personal
- flipping
- rent

Each type of rehabilitation may propose its own independent exit strategy, but these approaches are synonymous with each other.

The same basic principles of property renovation and improvement will continue to apply. However, for each type of rehabilitation, the way in which benefits are gained is slightly different.

A good way to think about it is to think about what the ultimate goal of the renovation is. Continue reading to learn about the rehabilitation of each type of property.

## PERSONAL

Personal rehabilitation looks exactly like that: the property is updated for personal use. This type of project is where the owner makes improvements for their own benefit.

They relate to functionality, aesthetics, and can even increase the value of the property. Personal rehabilitation is often referred to as a simple home renovation or renovation project.

Personal rehabilitation is a good starting point for homeowners interested in moving. Owners can learn the ropes while overseeing the renovation in their home before buying and refurbishing another home.

Personal rehabilitation is a great place to establish relationships with contractors and learn about job scope and project management. An additional benefit is the ability to perform personal rehabilitation without time constraints or other stress stresses.

Flipping

This popular rehabilitation strategy involves buying a home, renovating it, and immediately selling it to make a profit. The key to a successful change is often to ensure a reasonable purchase price, complete rehabilitation quickly, and minimize maintenance costs.

When it comes to changes, time is money. Completing changes in the shortest possible time is essential to reduce asset ownership and operational costs.

Investors interested in successfully changing their homes need to make sure that they understand the local market area and how it works. This strategy also requires practical knowledge of the industry and the rehabilitation process.

A good place to start moving is to follow another investor during the process. Ask your network mentor or other investors if they can include the following contracts.

This gives you a direct understanding of the importance of a good team, a quick timeline, and a healthy market.

# RENOVATION COMPONENTS

## INSPECT PROPERTIES BEFORE BIDDING

Impulse buying and the purchase of "invisible" properties are at serious risk, and inspection is necessary to properly assess the condition of the property and the repair budget. This provides a clear understanding of the number of funds required to complete the project and sold for profit successfully.

### THE INVERTED HOUSE IS MECHANICALLY BAD

Focus on new paints, new carpets, floors, trimmings, kitchenware, etc., where lower-cost improvements can have a major impact, and if your home has an old electrical system or the roof is leaking, rehabilitation costs are high, and you spend more on.

### PROFITABILITY IS PLANNED APPROPRIATELY

ROI should be calculated carefully and accurately and compared to the cost, including the holding period.

## PLAN DIFFERENT POTENTIAL EXIT STRATEGIES

The purpose of the flip is to make a profit immediately by selling. When spending exceeds the budget, such as raising funds or changing markets.

If you are forced to do so, a plan to hold and rent rather than lose is sometimes a better option. To do this, the purchase must be able to make money while having cash flow. If the answer is yes, it is a good purchase.

## ASSUMING WHO THE BUYER IS

In addition to this knowledge, you can know the ideal price and payment amount.

You just spend money on the effort to create a product that some-one in the market knows to buy.

## SELECT PROPERTIES THAT CAN BE UPDATED QUICKLY

The most important rule to keep in mind when trying to turn your house over is "time is money." You must select a property that can be updated immediately and sold immediately.

Many house fins use their borrowed money to buy real estate. If you have debt, it is essential to repay the loan before interest and fines are incurred. Even if you can't borrow money to buy, quick changes are always good for business.

## REACH A REPUTABLE HARD MONEY LENDER

When you find a property you want to change, it's time to purchase the house and raise money to make the necessary renovations. It is important to consider profit margins. Therefore, you should investigate your provider before you apply for a loan.

## UNDERSTAND RISK FACTORS AND DEVELOP A PLAN

Changing the house is a form of active investment. A successful real estate investor is someone who understands risk factors and knows how to eliminate or mitigate them effectively.

By understanding the risks associated with entering a property, you can plan specifically how to face the potential problems and collect the resources you need to deal with difficult times.

## KNOW THE ESTIMATED COST OF PULL

The first step in turning the house over is to understand the numbers. One of the most important figures is to determine the estimated cost of repair. You may need to pay real estate fees and certain closing costs.

If you borrow money to rent property taxes, utilities, insurance, interest, and a house, calculate all possible costs involved, including repair costs and other related costs.

## BUILD A GOOD REHABILITATION TEAM

Proper rehabilitation equipment is an important factor for first-time home buyers. Buyers should contact contractors and certified real estate inspectors, trusted real estate agents, and mortgage lenders. Reliable contractors can accurately assess what real estate needs and repair costs.

### CORRECTLY HOUSE PRICE

To change your home right away, you have to get the right price on your home when you are on the market. If you overestimate your home in an attempt to make the most money, you will simply stay on the market.

This is particularly attractive in the strong seller market when the property takes off the shelf. However, some investors suggest that you will get more money by conducting a bidding war than you would get if you set the house price appropriately and overestimated.

Once you set the right price, you will receive an offer within the first two weeks and will be able to sell the house as soon as possible.

## KNOW WHAT NEEDS TO BE IMPROVED

It is important to know what improvements are needed when building a house. There is a possibility of losing sales due to poor improvement of the property and increasing costs due to excessive improvement.

Be sure to check the refurbishments and repairs required for implementation and the following industry trends. If you have a budget that adds value to your home, incorporate the latest technology to improve heating, ventilation, air conditioning (HVAC), plumbing, electricity, appliances, and other smart homes.

### DON'T TRY TO BE TOO BIG

Don't try to be too big, especially if you're not familiar with the fixed and turnaround business. Start with a detached house and rehabilitation for less than $ 50,000.

Similarly, purchasing large real estate at large renovation investment costs is very dangerous, especially if it has just begun. It's better to start small while learning the rope

### DON'T MAKE UNNECESSARY IMPROVEMENTS

Modify only what is needed. Improving the property too much will not give you the expected return on investment (ROI).

Keep in mind that this is a business, and you are not renovating the house to look like a dream home. However, this rule is an exception, for example if you are repairing and turning a multi-million dollar house and this kind of change must be impressive.

## CHOOSE THE RIGHT MARKET

No, one thing is being in the right market. If you don't choose the right market, you will kill you in the first deal. Knowing the market can help in two ways. Make the right kind of updates that the market is ready to pay.

More importantly, it is likely that there are buyers waiting to purchase the final product. So do your homework and grow the area you want to turn. Since you have to travel several times a day, it is important to get close to home. You also need to select the best price range for flipping.

## DETERMINE THE AMOUNT OF CASH REQUIRED

In terms of home investment, investors with little investment experience looking for hard money lenders may need to get a lot of cash. Generally, this amount ranges from 20% to 40% of sales (down payment).

However, investors can reduce this amount by negotiating a contract in which the lender acquires a portion of the profit. If investors are experienced and have a good track record, hard money lenders are more likely to support little or no private money or a down payment from borrowers.

If the investor is new and has a small amount of money, it is necessary to get acquaintances such as family and friends to promise to collect some of the money and profits. Another option is to find a wealth of business partners who will pay you while you work.

## TAKE CARE OF ALL THE BIG ITEMS AND WORK CORRECTLY

An infamous stigma about house fins is that they tend to cut corners. He may sin for the association, but he can give bad names to those who are familiar with their work and who are thorough. Thank yourself and take care of all important items and work correctly for the first time. Potential buyers appreciate it and create a great reputation for your company to move forward in future deals. If you cut the corner, you can bite again.

## RENEWING VANITY

One of the most important improvements in repair and turning projects is the bathroom. When renewing a bathroom vanity, consider a natural colored floating vanity.

Soft and modern with rounded edges. The white quartz counter works in the bathroom. You can highlight them with a circular mirror. When selecting a cabinet color, consider shades and tones other than white. Natural nuts, mint, black and coal are successful. Sometimes white still works. Avoid shades of gray.

## ADD SOME HIGH-END FEATURES TO THE PROPERTY

Try adding high-end functionality to low-priced properties. For example, you can add a wall-mounted hood when you update your kitchen. The extra charge is between $ 100 and $ 200, but it is much more expensive. This allows you to sell your home at the best price and get higher profits.

# BUY THE WORST HOUSE IN THE BEST NEIGHBORHOOD YOU CAN AFFORD

"Worst" means a very poorly designed and outdated cosmetic form. Recoverable weathered hardwood, tremendous creative paint colors, disgusting carpets, unspoken scents, decades of builder kitchen cabinets, laminate or tile countertops, dirty toilets, and toilets please think about it. However, make sure you have a good foundation.

Unless you are an experienced renovator or contractor, it is essential that the entire floor, roof beams, columns, beams, and critical parts of the house's structural integrity are in excellent condition.

You may get involved in transaction theft due to the doneness of the house. You are looking for a home that you can get at a much lower price than the cleanest and most comparable house in the neighborhood.

List all the modifications and changes that need to be made and calculate the cost of them. Subtract this from the estimated value after the renovation of the house. This is a number that should not be passed.

## PLAN YOUR UPDATES CAREFULLY

Planning is one of the most important stages of agreement and change. This includes interviews with contractors and subcontractors and, if necessary, conversations with engineers and architects. Secure funding sources.

Review the process, schedule, and costs for obtaining permission in the county or city you plan to change. Next, create a timeline and a general budget. These must be customized according to the properties.

## INVESTIGATE THE LOCAL MARKET.

A detailed understanding of the local real estate market is important to the success of the project. For example, permission times and requirements vary widely from market to market, and requirements may change regularly.

Also, if you allow the problem, the project can be significantly delayed if not handled properly. In addition, the way you divide and categorize schools can vary widely, and knowing whether a house is in the desired school district can affect the final selling price of the house.

Proactively investigating local laws related to the real estate market and construction and comprehensive zoning can help alleviate these types of problems.

## TAKE THE NECESSARY REAL ESTATE COURSES

Because it is important to have the right type of education at the exchange, you need to take several courses, read books, and be familiar with business and terminology.

There is a lot to learn to become a professional in the repair and transformation business, including real estate auctions, working with contractors, finding the right projects for renovation, finding the right buyers.

## GET A GOOD CRM SYSTEM AND KEEP IT ORGANIZED

Learn how to get a good CRM system and use it effectively. Useful for organizing. Maintaining an organization is very important in the repair and exchange business because all transactions need to be on the right track and each team member must be on time. As a result, many unnecessary conflicts and emergencies can be avoided.

## FOCUS ON PAINTING, HARDWARE, AND LIGHTING.

Paint, hardware, and lighting are the best projects that provide ROI for home repair and turnaround. Simply update your lighting and hardware accessories throughout your home to take your flip project to the next level with minimal time and money.

## FIND A PROMISING NEIGHBORHOOD

Finding a region with a bright future but low prices can have good results. If there is new infrastructure development in the area, it is very likely that there will be a bright future.

For example, neighborhoods that are expanding streets or building new shopping centers are growing. Make an appropriate survey on the region's future development plans and select the right region.

## CHOOSE THE RIGHT MONEY LENDER

In addition to buying a home, you need money to repair the home and meet sales standards. Getting funding for solutions and changes can be difficult. Traditional lenders generally require full credit and often the process is long. It is better to find a lender that works with fins, has a simple application process, requires a small portion of the down payment, and has a quick response time.

## CONDUCT DUE DILIGENCE WHEN PURCHASING HIGHLY DIFFICULT PROPERTIES

Due diligence is very important when buying difficult real estate. Please make sure that the title of the property you are purchasing is free of lien and mortgage. Otherwise, calculate the risk associated with buying a property without a clear title and understand how to make decisions, liens, and code violations. Work with the most experienced title company in your area as it will help you navigate the process.

## WORK WITH REAL ESTATE AGENTS WHO KNOW THE LOCAL MARKET.

Speaking with professional real estate agents in the local market is very important to ensure profitable investment. Ask your real estate agent many questions about selling real estate. It's a mistake you don't want to underestimate the cost of closing in your area. If you do not accept closure costs, investigations, repairs, you can eat.

# CHAPTER NINE
# HOW TO ACCURATELY
# PRICE A HOME

## FOLLOW THE 10 PERCENT RULE

The PPSF numbers posted on the MLS do not take into account other factors. When performing a PPSF comparison, the 10% rule must be observed for accuracy.

The 10 percent rule states that both land improvement and area must be within 10 percent of the area of the property being assessed.

In other words, for a 2,000 square foot house on a 6,000 square foot property, the equivalent sales should be based on a lot of size property of 1,800-2,200 square feet, 5,400-6,600 square feet. The MLS number does not adjust the lot size.

To illustrate this point, if you are selling in Southern California, where the value is related to land rather than the size of the improvement, the calculation may fail completely if you do not consider the available lot size.

In other regions of the country where the lot value is very uniform, the price difference results from the difference in square feet coupled with the quality of improvement.

## THE TRUTH ABOUT IMPROVEMENT

Several commenters pointed out that the PPSF analysis does not consider upgrades. However, the data show that upgrades generally improve home sell-ability, but in most cases, add little or no real value.

The reason is as follows. How valuable are those beautiful new cherry wood cabinets when buyers try to tear them to replace them with white contemporary European cabinets?

There are some exceptions to this rule of thumb. Upgrades that add areas, such as additional bedrooms and additional baths, usually add value. For example, converting three bedrooms, one bath to four bedrooms, and two baths usually increases the value of the property.

## USE "THIRD"

If you perform a PPSF analysis over a long period of time, you can see that the actual prices are clustered into groups of about one third each. This varies, but the classification remains essentially the same.

Specifically, the best price PPSF is limited to the best conditions and best-located properties. The middle tier contains properties that are average values for the area.

That is, the lot size hovers around the area, area, and median of the area. The bottom third contains conditions, improvements, and / or properties whose location is not comparable to the top two thirds.

This is how it works for listing bookings: top layer properties are $ 170 to $ 182 per square foot, middle tiers are $ 145 to $ 162 per square foot, and bottom layers are $ 110 to $ 133 Suppose that Square feet. The current property comp is about $ 153 per foot. If the seller says they need the highest price per foot, use the following script:

"Mr. The seller and the wife are new or completely renewed for real estate sold for $ 170-182 per square foot. The real estate in this place with the same facilities as you currently has 1 They sell for $ 145-162 per foot.

"So if you want to sell for up to $ 182 per square foot, replace the kitchen, upgrade all bathrooms and change all dated fixtures to match what is currently available in that price range Otherwise, you can sell for $ 145-162 per square foot, it's your home and your decision, what you want to do. Do you want to sell at a lower price? "

## MARKET KNOWLEDGE IS STILL IMPORTANT

PPSF analysis works best when there is a solid basis for local values. The best agent can set the price of real estate accurately without consulting the equivalent sales. For example, if you start with a PPSF analysis of a high-rise apartment, you might add $ 10,000 per floor. South-facing city views require a $ 20,000 premium, and north-facing water views require a $ 50,000 premium.

There is no substitute for detailed market knowledge. Nevertheless, PPSF analysis continues to be a powerful and compelling tool not only for clients, but also for lenders, certified public accountants, and business managers. If you don't master this powerful tool, take time to do it. Coupled with strong market knowledge, it will almost always help keep the price right.

# CHAPTER TEN
# HOW TO CHOOSE A HOUSING CONTRACTOR

A remodeling plan was caught on a bench with a remodeling hat. So you are ready to put in a new tub, or you finally chose that new tile for your kitchen.

If you don't want to work on your own or if you don't have the time or skills to work on a DIY home improvement project, you might want to hire a contractor. However, choosing a contractor can be a headache. How can I tell if someone has a job that I don't know what to do?

When choosing a contractor, you are hiring a new employee for the job. You will not hire the first applicant for a job in your business, so do not select your home improvement contractor without narrowing down the best candidates.

Before making a final decision, examine the portfolio of previous works, verify the license, hear introductions, and collect competitive bids.

## GET RECOMMENDATIONS

The first step in finding a suitable housing improvement contractor is to create a list of 10-15 local contractors with the appropriate expertise. Gradually narrow this list to the top candidates and finally use it to select contractors. Therefore, it is recommended that you include more names than you need at this point.

- There are several ways to compile a starter list.
- Ask your homeowner friend, especially those who have recently been renovated, for recommendations.
- Search online for the type of service you need in your area.
- Check online review.
- Use social media to ask your friends and followers about local recommendations.

### Red flag

Successful contractors make it easy for you to contact them and see examples of their work. Beware of home renovators who lack basic information such as websites, social media presence, reviews, etc.

Contractor holding plan and tape measure

## COMPARE EACH CONTRACTOR'S PORTFOLIO

Choose a contractor specializing in the type of modification required. Those who specialize in kitchen remodeling may not be ideal for refurbishing your bathroom.

Home improvement contractors with creative eyes can also help with specific projects. For example, if you want to tile the entrance of a tile with a detailed mosaic, or if you want the room to be finished, you will need a contractor to do that type of work well.

Ask each contractor on the long list, at least for the portfolio of last year's projects. You may have a physical portfolio, or you may be directed to a website with images.

A good portfolio must contain at least 10 projects. You need to include photos of each space before starting work, during remodeling, and after completing the project. Useful if you have blueprints, sketches, or other plan photos so you can see how contractors approach your project.

**Red flag**

Look for a portfolio of images with too few projects, no pre-modification photos, and grainy and hard to see final products. Also note that home improvement contractors only include the best results in their portfolio. If completed projects do not meet the criteria, the average worker can be even worse. Remove the person's name from the list.

## ASK FOR LICENSE AND AUTHORIZATION

At this point, the list should have 6-8 names. One easy way to further refine is to seek contractor licenses and authorizations. The specific licenses or authorizations that a home improvement contractor should perform vary from project to project. Legal requirements vary from state to state, so contact your community's licensing department for specific requirements.

In addition to ensuring that the contractor has the correct license and authorization to complete the work safely and legally, the liability for liability if the listed person damages your home Make sure you have insurance.

Contractors and other workers are also eligible for worker compensation. Request a copy of the insurance and make sure it is up to date.

**Red flag**

Cross a contractor from a list that does not have the proper credentials. It is also advisable to mark off the names of people who are he or too long to get this information.

## CHECK REFERENCES

Now that you've narrowed the long list to the top 5-6 candidates let's start checking the references. Since this is a common practice, reputable contractors expect to request a reference list.

A typical contractor's reference list contains more than 10 jobs, including each customer's name, address, and phone number. Useful when each job has a date. If the dates are not in the list, ask them.

Let's call each reference. If the list is very long, select some recent projects and some old projects. Keep detailed notes during the call. You should ask for some references if you can go to their home to see the project directly.

There are some questions:

- Was the contractor on schedule?

- Has the job site been kept clean?
- Was the problem solved immediately?
- Is the contractor punctual on schedule and workday?
- How was your work postponed?
- Was the cost reasonable and clear?

**Red flag**

Some danger signals have too few references, or there is a large time difference between references. Ask these questions before assuming the worst. Calendar holes do not necessarily mean trouble. Maybe they were injured or taking a break. The openness and willingness of contractors to provide more information can help ease the mind.

If the client has a good overall experience, they will have a positive and positive attitude towards the contractor, even if there are some minor problems. If you don't have a good experience, you may find that the other person hesitates or answers indirectly. Read between the lines of what that person tells you.

They may not want to say unkind things. Eliminate contractors who get bad ratings or ambiguous reviews when discussing with each contractor's reference. At this point, you will be 3-4 contractors.

## CHECK THE COMPLETED PROJECT EXAMPLE

After calling the contractor's contact, cancel the low-rated contractor. Next, decide which of the remaining references to visit directly to see the contractor's completed project.

Choose an open and future-proof person that resembles your project and ideally lives near you. This is especially useful if work was completed at least a few years ago. Visit at least one completed project from each of the remaining top candidates.

Take a close look at the contractor's work when visiting the project. Ask if repairs or repairs are necessary. Check the overall feel and specific details.

**Red flag**

There are several red flags to look for, depending on the type of project.

- Bathroom modification: dark stains on walls or ceilings, sloping floors, inexpensive materials, insufficient lighting.
- Kitchen remodeling: obvious seams on countertops, inexpensive materials, "kitchen triangle" (stove, refrigerator, sink) not logically laid out, insufficient lighting, insufficient storage, or counter space.
- Paint: Paint overspray, paint runs, streaks, imperfect lines and edges, floor splatter.
- Tile work: curved tiles or lines, cracks in tiles or grouts, excessive grout or caulking along the edges (meaning to disguise imperfectly cut tiles), inconsistent grout lines, uneven surfaces, surfaces Clear transition between.
- Deck, patio or pergola: wavy or swollen boards, edge mismatch, gaps between boards or windows, cracks in floorboards, cracks or separation between sides of house and deck, cracks in concrete.

# GET A JOB BID AND HIRE A CONTRACTOR

To date, you have eliminated those who do extraordinary work from your list. The next step is to set the job price for all contractors that remain on the list.

After thorough consultations, each contractor presents a simple proposal for the project, called a bid, and an estimated cost. Depending on the type of renovation, the project timeline recommended material types, and total project cost details may be included. It is best to bid from the top 3-4 contractors on the list. Select a contractor from these bids.

Remember, it's not always best to go to the lowest price. In some cases, materials and workload may vary from contractor to contractor. For example, a contractor using a prefabricated cabinet will cost much less than a handcrafted woodworker, but you will notice that there are significant differences in the look and feel of the finished kitchen. When choosing which proposal is best for you, consider your overall goal of renovation.

After selecting a home center contractor and accepting the project bid, create a contract proposal with details on how to complete the project, timeline, materials, costs, and more. Once you confirm and sign the proposal, the project will proceed.

### Red flag

Beware of contractors trying to put pressure on accepting bids. Some contractors try to put pressure on signing immediately, saying that the bid is only valid for a limited period of time.

There is always an option to think about bidding for more than a few days. A quality contractor can spend time deciding which bid to choose and behaves gracefully even if a bid is declined. The same applies to the final contract. Be sure to check all details and do not sign anything immediately.

# CHAPTER ELEVEN
# REHABBING CONTRACTS

The first five important documents to discuss will be handed over to the rehabilitation contractor and will need to be signed and returned after the property is closed before construction begins. (It doesn't make sense to get a signature until you claim ownership.)

Under no circumstances should you submit the final document until the contractor has finished working on the project. Do not sign the final document until you are satisfied with all the deliverables of the rehabilitation project.

Also, have a real estate lawyer review the documents before handing them over. Even when using templates (especially when using templates). Be sure that you haven't missed anything.

## INDEPENDENT CONTRACTOR CONTRACT

This is the main binding contract that establishes the basic rules of the proposed relationship between the customer and the contractor. This is one of the most important things you can do to make the rehabilitation project go smoothly, as it outlines the main roles and responsibilities of each party in the transaction.

The contract covers licenses (contractor's responsibility), materials (select materials, contractor purchases materials), subcontractor use, work and completion schedule, arbitration role, insurance, etc. The

## WORKING RANGE

There may be no greater sign of your credibility, or lack thereof, than the final scope of work. Learning how to write a range of work is not difficult at all, but it is overwhelming for new investors.

Creating a real estate work scope requires the exact language, wording ambiguity, and specific deliverables, schedules, technical needs, summaries, and materials needed to confirm project completion.

There are several contractor work area templates, but whatever you use to create a work area, it is important to update it with the latest information. There is nothing that screams amateurs like the old work area, using the old work area template and using material information that refers to items that are no longer available.

## INSURANCE COMPENSATION

This is a stand-alone document that clearly defines the insurance requirements that a contractor must meet before starting work on a real estate rehabilitation project. This insurance coverage factor is also specified in the contract of the independent contractor, but it is recommended that the contractor agrees to these requirements in several places in the document.

This insurance requires more than just a signature. The contractor must include the following in the packet of documents:

Proof of liability insurance

Proof of workers' compensation insurance

Authentication from an insurance company (add an investment company as "additional insurance")

## PAYMENT SCHEDULE

The third document is the document that the contractor is most interested in and is clearly the payment schedule. This shows how the contractor is paid throughout the project. This is usually done through selected benchmarks, not contractors. It is important that both parties agree to this schedule before construction begins.

## W-9

The Internal Revenue Service (IRS) requires contractors who pay more than $ 600 within the calendar year to issue a 1099 form. To achieve this, every year, contractors must fill out a new W-9 form and collect information such as social security numbers and tax-payer numbers.

Needless to say, you need to fill out this W-9 before you start construction. If something goes wrong with the project and communication with the contractor goes wrong, it is almost impossible to obtain this kind of sensitive personal information after the fact.

## FINAL AND UNCONDITIONAL WAIVER OF LIEN

The final payment should not be sent to the contractor until all work is completed to satisfaction. However, after completing the final walkthrough and approving all deliverables shown in the scope of work, let the contractor sign the lien exemption, and have the contractor check.

Know that you performed the rehabilitation project in the most professional and experienced way, even if it was the first rehabilitation real estate project.

## MANAGING YOUR REHAB

How to perform real estate rehabilitation

Fortunately, learning how to complete real estate rehabilitation is not as complicated as it seems. Although preparation and effort are required, following these steps can ensure the success of the rehabilitation facility.

- Walkthrough the properties to get a better idea of what needs to be done.
- Create a work area that outlines the details of the rehabilitation project.
- Find the right contractor for the job.
- Organize important documents and get ready to get started.
- Manage all aspects of rehabilitation projects.
- Complete another walkthrough and make the final payment for the job.

- Stage properties and host open houses.

PREPARE / CREATE PLAN

Starting a rehabilitation project requires more than a rough look at the necessary refurbishment and contractor employment. First, you need to evaluate your property carefully. This ensures that all aspects of the real estate construction process are on the course. When creating a plan, there are two things that need to be determined.

Necessary repairs: Bring your camera, graph paper, and measurement tools with you during your visit. These are useful for gathering a more detailed evaluation of a property. Take a picture of the problem area and measure the exact repairs you need. Your photos can also give you front and back shots to show your clients. Take flashlights in dark corners and rooms.

Improvements to help sell your home: Are there certain rooms that need more sunlight? It may be helpful to install large windows or skylights. Do I need to install carpet or flooring? How about color and style? Note the improvements that increase the value of the property.

When finished, create a sketch of the properties. This time, the repair and improvement items you want to see are divided into items up to the last square meter. This will help communicate your vision to the contractor.

Bonus tip: Every time a contractor visits, having a lockbox and a spare key at the facility doesn't make the investor go straight and give the investor a bad idea. Save time by not having to meet each time you need access to the facility.

## CREATING A WORK AREA

The scope of work largely depends on the plan before rehabilitation. This is the place where the contractor details the scope of the project to see all major or minor renovations. To do this successfully:

Read through the planning notes and list all the necessary modifications (destruction, removal, floor installation, etc.).

To make your budget more efficient, prioritize each renovation as "needed," "want," or "optional."

Estimate the cost of each project. If the budget is exceeded, the optional ones can be abolished.

Everything you need to do every repair or refurbishment, from the last fixture, faucet, and furniture. Also, look at reusable materials instead of buying new ones.

Establish work scope based on cost estimates for each project. Remember to always budget for unexpected problems.

The final scope of work will be presented to future contractors, who will bid.

Don't forget to compare the value of the home after renovation with what is available in the neighborhood. Buyers avoid your property if you sell at a higher price than the current rate.

## HIRE A CONTRACTOR

Contractors make rehabilitation projects easy or difficult. It is important to spend time when choosing contractors to share real estate rehabilitation contracts.

You can find contractors through investor networks, websites, job boards, local building departments, suppliers, or local real estate associations.

The first step is to create specialized documentation that will help you sell yourself to potential contractors. This includes your own background, your goals (will they be able to work with you again in the future?), The kind of relationships you can expect from working with you, and what you are looking for in contractors It is If possible, include how the previous project was processed (eg, payment schedule, work scope, etc.).

These details will help you build trust and establish a reputation as a trusted real estate rehab. Make sure your pitch shows you as a viable business partner, not only for this project but also for future business partners.

Pre-screening interviews can help assess the suitability of contractors. I have a few questions:

- Years of experience
- Owned equipment
- Team workers
- Licenses and permissions
- insurance
- Subcontractor
- bankruptcy
- Willingness to provide future referrals

## IMPORTANT DOCUMENTATION AND INTRODUCTION

Once you have evaluated and selected the best contractor for your rehabilitation project, you can proceed to sign the contract. Do not start the project until all relevant parties have accepted and signed the agreement. (This is mandatory.)

Make sure that the document has the following:

Independent Contractor Contract: All details about the project, including price.

Scope of work: details of project scope and limitations. Includes all materials used.

Payment details: When payment is delivered.

Insurance compensation form: insurance requirements for contractor workers and responsibilities during the project period.

W-9 Tax Form: This is the form that IRS needs for an independent contractor.

Final waiver: This is at the end of the project, but it is best first to provide the contract to the contractor.

Once the form is ready, schedule a meeting and discuss with all interested parties (contractors, subcontractors). This gives you the peace of mind that everyone involved is on the same page, especially the project details, duration, and budget. Entertain proposals and deal with disputes immediately.

MANAGEMENT OF REHABILITATION

When you are in the real rehabilitation ditch, you encounter five different (but important) stages:

Demolition and garbage cleanup: Removal of damaged items (walls, floors, toilets, plumbing, etc.). External cleanup includes dead trees, bushes, fences, decks and more.

Foundation and framing issues: At this stage, the house skeleton is processed.

HVAC, plumbing, electricity: After this stage, a building inspector will come to check that the installation is correct.

Insulation: Remember to start insulation only after the electrical and piping inspection is complete. Depending on your current location, you need to make sure that the wiring, piping, and ducts are properly hidden.

Trimming and painting: Trimming following painting is part of the final stage of rehabilitation. You now begin to see your vision come back to life.

Walk-through inspection and final payment

There are a few things that you may not notice no matter how careful you are and how much you trust the contractor. To provide this, you must perform a second walkthrough of the property after all initial checks are complete.

Make sure that the contractor has provided everything listed in the contract. Also, remember that a final inspection is required to finalize the building permit. (Budget time for this)

If you find the project satisfactory, create a Lien final waiver letter to be signed by the contractor. Make final payments for good jobs quickly (and lay the foundation for future work relationships).

STAGING (OPEN HOUSE)

You have come a long way, but now is the time to sell your home. This means cleaning the house and getting ready for staging. Staging provides potential buyers with ideas on how to efficiently use available space in real estate.

Stage bathroom, master bedroom, kitchen, and living room; let them think about what happens when you live in this house. Also make sure that the exterior can be presented equally (lawn, fence, etc.). Needless to say, professional photos help sell your home faster than photos taken from smartphones or real estate that have no photos at all.

I would like to think about how to leave a good lasting impression on potential buyers. Where should we spread the word to attract more potential customers? What can you do to close a deal?

Allow potential home buyers to imagine themselves at your rehabilitation facility, and you are already doing most of the hard work.

REHABILITATION FACILITY

Overview

Rehab investor journeys can be daunting, especially if you don't already have a lot of real estate rehabilitation contracts. However, by dividing the house flipping process into seven main stages, you can see that the fix and flip investors do not try to do everything at once.

They have a vision of the whole picture. At the same time, they are paying attention to the daily progress of rehabilitation. They certainly know one thing. By doing due diligence and arming with information, there is nothing they can't handle.

# HOW TO PROPERLY BUDGET FOR REHABILITATION

Performing repairs with real estate rehabilitation investments can be more time consuming than other aspects of the project it is also your biggest expense and often will be higher than the actual purchase price of the real estate

As a result, it is important to have a proper budget for repairs in advance, so the final result is not surprising. Use the following tips from Catalyst Funding experts to prepare for your success.

A good rehabilitation budget starting with a comprehensive form

Make sure you have a budgeting form that you can bring to every home you visit. You can print this form on paper or find a smartphone app that suits your needs. The important thing is that if you choose to proceed with the project, make sure that the form contains all the information, you need to make a budget throughout the process.

Get in and out of the form and make sure you can easily calculate the price so that you can get through the house efficiently while being thorough and not missing anything.

To get the best deal when buying from wholesalers and homeowners, you need to move very quickly. By filling your budget on the fly, you can decide whether a deal is right for you and make an offer as soon as possible before another investor can beat you.

## WHAT TO INCLUDE IN THE REHABILITATION BUDGET FORM

You may want to make sure it is on the form so that you don't forget. Common categories to include the following:

- Basic repair
- Roofing
- Paint (both inside and outside)
- Flooring
- Electrical
- Plumbing
- Bathroom fixtures
- Kitchen cabinets and appliances
- Door and window
- Heating and air conditioning
- Landscaping and cleanup
- Carpentry

## HELPFUL TIPS FOR CALCULATING REHABILITATION BUDGETS

When creating and filling out budget forms, reduce as many items as possible to the price per square foot. This saves you time walking through the house. A smaller, more focused approach can help you find small things that can be missed, such as plugs, switches, doorknobs, door stops, and so on.

Also, paying attention to details can help you determine what can be left as is, what can be reused with minor repairs, and what needs to be completely replaced.

Preparing a budget form on the spot will allow you to make a quick offer at the property, but it is always wise to know the exit strategy before you first visit the house.

What happens if something happens and I can't start the rehabilitation project on time? Can I wholesale my assets to another real estate investor? What happens if I have a problem selling my home after completing the rehabilitation work? Can I rent until the property is sold? With a backup plan in mind, the stress on the entire rehabilitation project is greatly reduced.

○

# CHAPTER TWELVE
# HOME STAGING
# THE HOME STAGING COST

Hire a house stager. A professional house stager not only decides which of your belongings need to be sorted and moved from the home before putting it on the market but also undertakes which project to maximize the final selling price from repainting. You will also be able to determine the dining room for installing a new cabinet door in the kitchen.

Note that home service information sites and marketplace HomeAdvisor cost an average of $ 822 to hire a home stager or decorator for staging purposes, but in the high end this service can cost up to $ 2,500 .

Many stagers can help provide information by providing a flat-rate consultation, which usually costs hundreds of dollars, but can be thousands of dollars if there are fully staged vacant properties.

Like everything related to a home sale, the price of a home stager depends on location, demand, and the amount of assistance needed. Simple advice to make sure your home is ready for an open house is much cheaper than a thorough staging by a professional team.

Save extra belongings. One of the biggest lessons behind staging is to tidy up the house. It not only removes the miscellaneous paper on the kitchen table, cleans children's toys scattered in the living room, but also reduces the number of books on the shelf, replaces the oversized section with a small sofa and closet Take out clothes from.

If you haven't moved from your home yet, you have no room to hide your extra belongings. Rent a nearby storage unit "to put furniture and other things there."

Depending on how much you need to move and where you live, storage units can be expensive in months. However, stuffing a garage or backyard shed can make buyers look like potential buyers and can be turned off if you cannot see them when you tour the house.

## RENTAL OF FURNITURE

Many professional stagers own furniture to rent while the house is on the market. Or you can rent from a local furniture location while a real estate agent is showing your home.

If renting furniture all the time your home is on the market doesn't fit your budget, consider at least a more ideal, rented furniture for marketing photography, free up space or work more conservatively Then return to the tour staging. Home photos are just as important as tours, as almost all home buyers start searching online.

## WHICH ROOM DO I NEED TO STAGE

Stand out in the buyer's heart

If you still live at home, you need to stage all the rooms where you live. If you have all the extra furniture and take-away items in your room, you won't be aware that the buyer is visiting the facility.

Be careful about the room you enter first because the first impression is the most important.

Enter from your front door instead of side doors or garages, because the front of your home will give the buyer a first impression. By getting into the habit of entering from the front, you are more likely to notice extra shoes on the foyer, no longer functioning doorbells, or burnt-out porch lights.

## HERE IS A BREAKDOWN OF THE MOST COMMON ROOMS TO STAGE

**Kitchen:** Home buyers primarily view the kitchen not only as a place for cooking but also as a social venue. Don't have too many coffee makers, mixers and cookbooks at the counter. However, the kitchen table and breakfast bar should be set up to prepare for snacks and brunch.

**Bathroom:** Guest and master bathrooms are important. Keep all toothbrushes, shampoos, and soaps out of sight. That way, no buyers are thinking about getting ready early in the morning. To organize the room, prepare a clean bath mat and towel according to the color scheme.

**Living room:** A common area is important for imagining how home buyers spend their spare time. Keep all furniture in the right size so that space feels spacious even if it's not the largest room.

**Master bedroom:** Always make a bed and add pillows and fluffy comforters to make it look like a comfortable space. Do not put laundry on the floor. Do not keep it all in your closet. Morales says he wants more storage space in the house, so "at least half of what is it is closed."

**Tricky room:** Strangely shaped dining rooms and small side rooms can benefit from staging and help buyers understand how to use the room successfully, even if it is not the primary room the home buyer cares about The For example, instead of having a queen-size bed in a small bedroom, a double bed can emphasize space.

When still living at home. If your family is still at home during marketing, you can stage the space, but it may require additional organization. Extra bedrooms in vacant homes may not be staged, but when living there, clean up children's toys, do not block windows, make the room bigger, and bunk beds or babies as much as possible Consider placing the bed as far as possible from the door.

## HOME STAGING TIPS

Please remove your own style. You may have an lectrical taste, but your buyer may not. "Suggestions may not be your personal taste or style, but it is not a point. In many cases, there are recommendations for classic and simple side staging errors using neutral and occasional accent colors.

A seat that can be distracting, you may think that there is a bit of habit or that the bright colors will be the happiest at home, but that's not the way everyone operates, but you want to focus on attracting as many potential buyers as possible.

Less is better. It's not just the other messy people walking down the street. Even if your home is clean, there are some mess you can do. According to the Home Staging Report of the National Association of Real Estate Agents, the agent has no

Don't forget that "First View" is online: I always tell the seller that your first show is a virtual show. Therefore, it is a priority to have a good photo and introduce your home in the best possible way. Less and larger items introduce space and give a larger scale so buyers can visualize themselves at home. A bright and tidy space will help you take better photos, increase the number of time buyers see your home, and lead to faster sales.

**Add luxury with the great bed linen**

Beds tend to be the center of most bedrooms, so don't settle for just the linen your clients have. Luxury duvets, pillows, throws, and siamese collections are the keys to an effective bedroom. If you want to see how important bed linen is for staging your house, along with excellent lighting and composition, see the following shots before and after.

## Create a command station

One area we are constantly focusing on is the creation of "command stations." This space needs storage space (filing, cabinets, bins, and baskets all work). Simple desks and seats highlight both the shape and function of space and present options that the buyer has never thought of. Now the new owner can sit there and manage his life and create the home he wants.

### Replace old light fixture

What are my best tips for staging a house? Let's have light. Renewing lighting fixtures makes a big difference in almost every space. This is especially true for non-newly built homes. One of the greatest gifts of the house era is the outdated lighting fixtures. We recommend that you replace the old luminaire with a more modern luminaire and add a balance between floor and table lamps to brighten the room. To achieve a truly cost-effective solution, natural light can also be taken from the windows. If a better buyer can see the house, they can see the house better.

### If in doubt, bring a professional stager

I am a professional home stager, and most agents suggest that you clean and tidy up. Unfortunately, most of the sellers don't know what it really means, so they go too far to the point of sterilization.

There are fine lines. If an agent or seller doesn't know how to see the house the buyer wants, it is always best to call a professional to achieve the best possible look at the house. Agents are negotiating professionals, not necessarily home aesthetics.

### Try Flash staging

One of the tricks we have done with past properties is "flash staging." A staging company and a professional real estate photographer come in, take the house to the stage, do thorough professional photography, and remove all furniture and decorations. It all takes hours because the same furniture and decoration can be continuously reused in different homes. Much cheaper than traditional staging

### Always give purpose to the room

If you don't know what to do with the room, there will be no potential buyers, and your home will be remembered as having a kitchen and everywhere that interesting space!

Remove the coat from the front closet, remove excess Tupperware from the pantry, and keep the magazines off the coffee table. You might host one or two Thanksgiving in the dining room, but if 6 pairs feel like a complete set, you don't need to place all 10 legs around the table. Move these items to storage, family garages, or sell them to reduce the load before moving.

Please clarify the route. When selling furniture side by side, the goal is to make each room look spacious and emphasize the simple and wise flow from room to room. Each room has a clear path for homebuyers to walk from door to door and avoid tripping over protruding side tables, chairs, and rugs.

These relocations can mean that the sofa is not properly positioned for ideal television viewing. If you need to unplug the TV and go to another place or storage in the room to highlight a partially covered image window, remember the best features of the room instead of furniture to help.

Delete personal items. Part of the tidy process includes removing all family photos, religious symbols, and other personal items from view. If there is a child's school portrait on the upper floor wall, the buyer will imagine that the child is enjoying the house instead of his own.

Not only that, but buyers sometimes struggle to get rid of prejudice when traveling home, so keep tips on your race, religion, and nationality private and avoid all possible discrimination, please.

Please basically. Keep the same simple and classic theme in mind, from wall colors to furniture styles. "Accent walls need to be repainted neutral so that the color doesn't distract potential buyers. You want to make your home ready to move, and blank canvases are buyers Is a way to imagine how your art and furniture will look at home.

While neutral colors and traditional appearance may seem boring, the point of staging is to see the potential of the space rather than providing a concrete suggestion about how the room should be Is to be able to do it. Since every individual has their own style, it is best not to choose a wall color that seems too bright for potential buyers or to include a large antique chaise lounge that makes it difficult to remember the rest of the room .

Always be prepared to display. If the stager moves to new furniture, the house staging will not stop. The house must always be ready for the tour. This means there are no dishes in the sink, no homework on the dining table, and no wet towels on the floor.

## 1. Save money with virtual staging

Staging your home helps you sell vacant listings at a higher price, but hiring a professional staging company can be expensive. In addition, many solo agents and small real estate teams do not have the budget and other resources to purchase and store a variety of home-style furniture.

With this platform, you can schedule professional photography and personalize your listing photos with a number of beautiful templates, including virtual furniture, rugs, lamps, wall art, and other decorations.

## 2. Prepare clients mentally

In my opinion, the first and most important step to selling a home is to prepare my clients for the future mentally. When selling a house, it is important for the seller to understand that his home no longer feels like his home.

Some owners may find it difficult to hide their children's toys and their belongings that they use every day before the screening or to clean up odd heirlooms on display (which may be the easiest to see maybe) however, it explains the benefits and importance of keeping your home neutral, tidy and tidy. This is a potential pitfall when occupying a house.

## 3. Staging does not cover the house

I once showed apartments with sexually explicit artwork throughout the house. Not surprisingly, it was all my buyers remembered from the apartment. They were distracted by the art, so they didn't notice the big kitchen or the amazing scenery.

I want to highlight the superior quality of the house, not the furniture or art. In many cases, furniture and artwork are the first items a buyer will notice first, so the furniture needs to be simple and unobtrusive.

Use neutral colors such as white and beige for furniture and walls. Finally, add pop colors to pillows, table lamps, artwork, and other accessories to make them stand out in your photos.

# CHAPTER THIRTEEN
# BUYER DUE DILIGENCE

As a seller, you often get nervous during the home inspection process. We don't want to be bound by the cost and burden of repairs if the deal doesn't close, or the buyer demands them in the unlikely event. Fortunately, there are a few things you can do to prepare for the exam.

**Provides open access to areas that need to be checked**

Make sure that home inspectors have easy access to the entire property. If an area cannot be reached, it cannot be inspected. This is dangerous for buyers. Remove confusion that prevents access to areas or systems that inspectors need to examine, such as basements, attics, furnace rooms, and sinks.

**Clear the border**

In addition to checking the functionality of your home's interior, the inspector will also examine the appearance of siding, trim, and caulking around windows and doors. Leave your house in a place free of plant growth, trash, and stored items to keep out of the way.

## Check the roof

When did you often look at the roof of your house? For most sellers, it's been a while. However, the roof is an important part of the house inspection, so you cannot ignore it when preparing. Take out the ladder, clean the mess and debris in the gutter, check for damaged or missing tiles, and make sure the down dropper is in the correct position. If damage is found on the roof, you may want to take care of the roof before inspecting the house.

## Keep a clean house

If you have already experienced the process of selling a house, you are probably quite used to cleaning everything up at this point. After an accepted offer, resist the urge to build things up and maintain the same level of cleanliness for home inspectors. Cleaning the house does not affect the inspection itself, but if the house is dirty or dirty, it may cause the inspector to suspect that other areas of the facility are not properly managed.

## If the bulb is burnt out, replace it

If a light bulb breaks, it suggests two things to the home inspector. Either the bulb is burned out, or there is something wrong with the wiring of the fixture. The inspector simply finds that the fixture is either time consuming to determine if it is inoperable or that it may be defective without further investigation. Make sure that all bulbs are functioning properly and avoid both of these scenarios.

## Make sure the toilet is functioning properly

Does your toilet run for a long time after you flush? This is a common problem that is often ignored when living together every day but is not something you want to show to your home inspector.

Repairing the running toilet is a simple and inexpensive repair and can be handled by a simple trip to the hardware store, so handle the problem before the inspection.

## Put in a new furnace return filter

Regular replacement of home furnace filters is important for air quality and the overall functioning of the heating system. Pay attention to the inspector by cleaning or replacing the existing filter instead of worrying about not enough heat and air in the house.

## Turn on all pilot lights

The water heater pilot light is probably always on (if you haven't already), what about the gas fireplace pilot light? Many homeowners turn off the fireplace during warm months. It is therefore important to reconfirm that the pilot lights and the fireplace itself are functioning before the inspection. If you turn off the pilot light on the fireplace, now is the time to light the fire again.

## Make sure the fuse box is properly labeled

Misleading fuse boxes can be frustrating for homeowners and home inspectors. Double-check that each switch in the box is clearly and accurately labeled and replace any incorrect or difficult-to-read labels.

## Check the door

Walk around the house and check each door to make sure it is in working condition. Indoor and outdoor doors should be latched into the frame without problems, and the doorknob should be securely fastened. In particular, door locks leading to the outside must also function properly. From time to time, cold and heat can distort properly functioning doors and cause problems, so check all doors, including those that you do not use frequently.

**Repair a broken cabinet**

The cabinet hinges are slightly looser, so the door will not close properly or will be flush with the frame. If you have a cabinet looking down, it is usually fairly easy to fix by simply tightening the hinge with a screwdriver.

**Find leaks and floods**

Home inspectors are surely looking for signs of leaks and flooding, so it is recommended that they are defeated and repair water-related problems prior to testing. When looking for leaks, be sure to check under the sink, around the faucet, around the toilet / tub / shower base, and under potentially leaking equipment such as a dishwasher or refrigerator.

For water damage, examine the walls, ceiling, and floor for signs of warping, sagging, or buckling. Don't forget to check the exterior of the house for signs of leaks and water damage. If you see water near the base of your house, it should be a cause for concern.

**Beware of bug issues**

Most of us sometimes have to deal with false ants and spiders in the house, especially at warm temperatures. However, if there is a hornet's nest in the backyard, or if you regularly see ant rows in the kitchen or another interior area, you will need to address these issues before inspection. Most bug issues aren't a big deal, but you can disable buyers.

**Please prepare on the day of the inspection**

By the day of your home exam, everything you can do to prepare should be complete. Well, that is to make sure it goes as smoothly as possible. To do so, leave all utilities on and double-check that there is clear access to areas and systems throughout the house, and keep gates, electrical boxes, or other areas that are normally kept safe.

Release the lock. Best of all, get ready (known early) at least two hours before the inspector arrives, and prepare yourself and your family to leave the house during the test. We recommend that you bring your pet with you, but if you can't, make sure you can safely put it in a cage or store it safely.

Take a deep breath at this point. Most buyers do not expect complete completion. They just want to know that there is no big burden waiting for them. Home inspectors are usually aware of a few small problems, but in most cases, if you already need to detect something serious, you already know it yourself.

# CLOSING

THE CLOSING PROCESS

The closing process for sellers

Negotiation

Be prepared for negotiations, as the merchant closing process begins when the offer begins to enter. Even if the offer is the offer price, you can still counter-offer, especially if there are multiple offers on the table.

When a buyer makes an offer to your property, you have three choices: you can accept the terms as they are, and you can cancel and modify some terms.

Counteroffers are most often used. It's like a tennis match between you and your prospect. Each ball returning to your court will tell you something. Are buyers serious about price? If you are not moving at a price or moving slowly, you need to accept or reject the price. After one or two exchanges with little price fluctuation, the buyer does not move. At this point, it is up to you to accept or reject their offer.

Try to understand the motives of buyers who buy real estate. If you understand these, you may be able to negotiate terms other than price. Shorten inspection and termination schedules. You can also pay a transfer tax or title fee for the seller. Ask to cover a certain amount of repairs that may come from the inspection. There are many ways to offer better offers without renegotiating prices.

During the negotiations, keep your emotions down and do nothing personally. Even after a contract is signed, it may be necessary to favor it before signing the contract. I didn't want to deal with an angry buyer because I was uncomfortable before.

If the table has multiple offers, you can take advantage of this by playing offers with each other. Returning to each potential buyer and telling them that a higher and better offer is needed, they are given the opportunity to raise the offer price and reduce or eliminate contingencies. Set the best offer and the date and time to accept the best offer. If someone is actually interested in the property, they will respond on time.

Once all offers have been collected, consider all contingencies in addition to the offer price. Unforeseen circumstances, such as closures that are conditional on the sale of another home, can cause problems. If you have a low-priced offer that doesn't have this type of randomness, you should seriously consider it.

Do not rush to negotiate the contract. Do not drag too much. Ideally, this part of the closure process should take a few days. Longer than that, the buyer may lose interest and decide that it is difficult to deal with. Please do everything you agree in writing and make sure that both parties sign the sales agreement.

**Financial expenses and taxes**

Make sure you know the cost of closing the seller. How do they affect your earnings? You will also borrow government money from this transaction. How much do you know

If the ownership of real estate is transferred during the process of closing a seller's house, the cost of closing both buyers and sellers can be substantial. Sellers typically have to pay real estate brokerage fees, closure fees, ownership fees, some transfer taxes, all outstanding school taxes, and property taxes incurred during the period of ownership.

Several other unexpected costs, mainly fees, can also cut into the bottom line. Prepare to be liable for lien release, mortgage prepayment penalties, recording fees, notary fees, escrow fees, attorney fees, and repairs. Many sales contracts include seller concessions, which are also displayed as commissions.

Costs vary greatly from state to state and vary from state to state, so costs cannot be estimated. Note that they can be important. If you have a real estate agent, ask them to estimate all-inclusive closure costs from the beginning. Please note what is included in the quote. As a result, you can adjust estimates when negotiating various incidents with potential buyers.

You should also find out what your tax obligation is from the sale as soon as possible. Some states require all off-state sellers to withhold certain profits from the settlement. Other states require title companies to report profits. As a seller, you are taxable at both state and federal levels for profits derived from your flips. Knowing about state and local tax laws, it is best to consult a local accounting professional with real estate experience.

**Agent percentage**

Agents always get a share of sales. What is the correct ratio? Should I negotiate?

If you bring a real estate agent to the home change team, depending on where you are in the United States. In the US, real estate agents are usually paid between 5% and 7% of the sale price of real estate. You 'll need to do your own research to find the right price in your area. Generally, the seller pays the agent's fee. If there are buyers and sellers, the commission is divided between them. Note that even though it looks like a lot of money, the agent is not paid for the job until the property is successfully sold.

You can negotiate lower agent fees, but that's not always a good idea. If the agent has a property to show to buyers, will he push what they pay cheaper? If an agent has several lists that need an open house, does he spend an afternoon on a property that pays him the minimum amount of his list? of course not. You can save money by negotiating a low commission, but in reality, it costs a lot because the agent is not careful.

If you really want to get the agent's attention, offer a bonus for selling real estate. Increasing commissions by 1% can also draw the attention of trading agents and may result in faster sales.

## Closing

Sign the document and transfer the file. Make sure there are no errors. What do you do if there is? Do you need a lawyer? What does the title company do when closing?

Simply put, closing is when a buyer gives money to a seller in exchange for ownership. Buyers and sellers must participate in closing with real estate agents, closing agents, and lawyers (if that is the custom of the country)

If no lawyer is present, obtain all final documents in advance. If you are unfamiliar or experienced with this, but this transaction is more complex than usual, be sure to check with your lawyer and all documents before closing, so you know what you are signing and accepting .

There are payment sheets that categorize the costs paid by buyers and sellers. You need to indicate how much the buyer needs to bring to the closing table and how far away the seller should be. Make sure the assignment is correct and complies with the terms of the sales contract. You need to get a share.

Once the close process is complete and the document has been signed, make sure that the amount of the check drawn matches the amount outstanding on the payment sheet. If not, do not leave it until it matches. The payment sheet is a legal record of the transaction and must be accurate.

The title agency you are dealing with has already reviewed the title history of the property and would probably eliminate the existing title issue. They are parties that are actually due. The title agent is the person responsible for ensuring that all numbers match, collecting the appropriate signature and notary, and issuing a check. The closing process can run smoothly or fall into a nightmare. The title company is also responsible for registering the land transfer certificate with the local government and registering the buyer's mortgage with the bank.

# CONCLUSION

When it comes to real estate, there are tons of ways to make money, and flipping houses is a great place to start. Flipping homes can be very lucrative, as long as you know how to go about it.

If you're serious about getting into the business of flipping houses, then this is the book for you. It's designed specifically to help you avoid the dangers that could eat into your profits, and will teach you to recognize the more desirable properties so you can be the first to snatch them off the market.

House flipping is not easy. There are many competitions. It costs money. It takes time, and things are always more expensive than you think. Projects always take longer than expected.

You can get frustrated, trying to flip the first house. If it takes months or longer to find and purchase the first property, you must stick.

Once purchased, it may not proceed as planned. But you must continue to treat difficult times as learning experiences. With every flip you do, you learn how to make it better.

By sticking to disciplined flipping rules, you can make a profit by flipping in a slow or rapidly valued market. Because of this short-term way of investing in real estate, the flipping of housing is considered immune to extreme market fluctuations.